·VOICES·
from
COLONIAL AMERICA

NEW JERSEY

ROBIN DOAK
WITH

BRENDAN McCONVILLE, PH.D., CONSULTANT

NATIONAL GEOGRAPHIC

WASHINGTON, D.C.

One of the world's largest nonprofit scientific and educational organizations, the National Geographic Society was founded in 1888 "for the increase and diffusion of geographic knowledge." Fulfilling this mission, the Society educates and inspires millions every day through its magazine, books, television programs, videos, maps and atlases, research grants, the National Geographic Bee, teacher workshops, and innovative classroom materials. The Society is supported through membership dues, charitable gifts, and income from the sale of its educational products. This support is vital to National Geographic's mission to increase global understanding and promote conservation of our planet through exploration, research, and education.

For more information, please call 1–800–NGS LINE (647–5463) or write to the following address:

NATIONAL GEOGRAPHIC SOCIETY
1145 17th Street N.W.
Washington, D.C. 20036–4688
U.S.A.

Visit the Society's Web site at www.nationalgeographic.com.

John M. Fahey, Jr., *President and Chief Executive Officer*
Gilbert M. Grosvenor, *Chairman of the Board*
Nina D. Hoffman, *Executive Vice President, President of Books and Education Publishing Group*
Ericka Markman, *Senior Vice President, President of Children's Books and Education Publishing Group*

STAFF FOR THIS BOOK

Nancy Laties Feresten, *Vice President, Editor-in-Chief of Children's Books*
Suzanne Patrick Fonda, *Project Editor*
Bea Jackson, *Art Director, Children's Books*
Janet A. Dustin, *Illustrations Coordinator*
Carl Mehler, *Director of Maps*
Justin Morrill, *The M Factory, Inc., Map Research, Design, and Production*
Connie D. Binder, *Indexer*
Rebecca Hinds, *Managing Editor*
R. Gary Colbert, *Production Director*
Lewis R. Bassford, *Production Manager*
Alan V. Kerr and Vincent P. Ryan, *Manufacturing Managers*

Voices from Colonial New Jersey was prepared by CREATIVE MEDIA APPLICATIONS, INC.

Robin Doak, *Writer*
Fabia Wargin Design, Inc., *Design and Production*
Matt Levine, *Editor*
Susan Madoff, *Associate Editor*
Laurie Lieb, *Copyeditor*
Laurie Lieb, *Proofreader*
Jennifer Bright, *Image Researcher*

Body text is set in Deepdene, sidebars are Caslon 337 Oldstyle, and display text is Cochin Archaic Bold.

LIBRARY OF CONGRESS CATALOGING-IN-PUBLICATION DATA

Doak, Robin S. (Robin Santos), 1963–
    New Jersey / Robin Doak with Brendan McConville.
        p. cm. — (Voices from colonial America)
    Includes bibliographical references and index.
    ISBN 0–7922–6385–5 (Hardcover)
    ISBN 0–7922–6680–3 (Library)
    1. New Jersey—History—Colonial period,
ca. 1600–1775—Juvenile literature. I. McConville,
Brendan, 1962– II. Title. III. Series.
    F137.D59 2005
    974.9'02—dc22
                                            2004026242

Printed in Belgium

CONTENTS

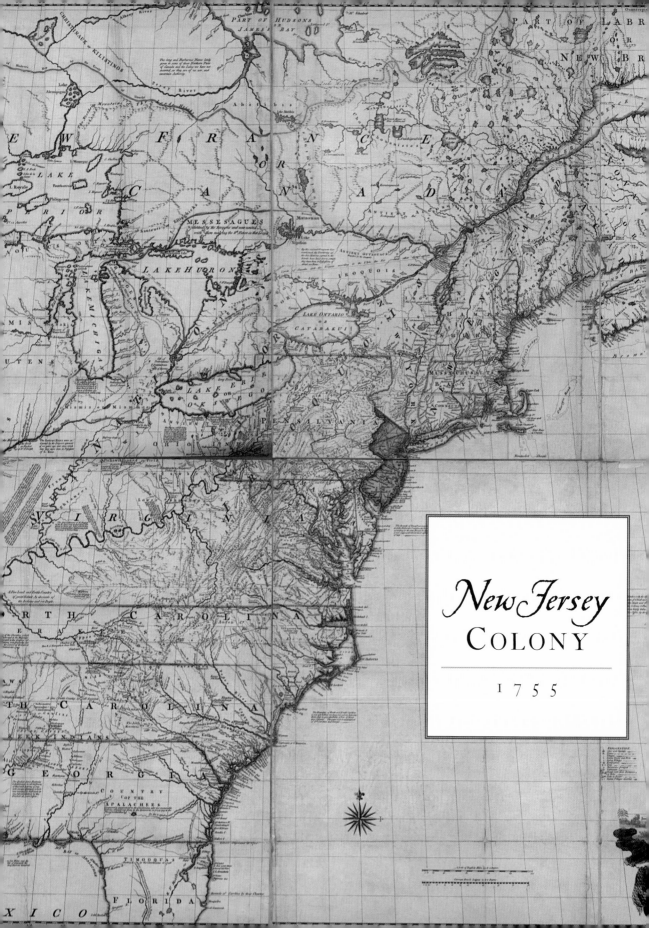

New Jersey
COLONY

1755

INTRODUCTION

by

Brendan McConville, Ph.D.

This 1764 engraving shows the College of New Jersey,
which later became the famed Princeton University.

To read the words of those who visited or lived in colonial
New Jersey is to understand the differences that separated
their world from our own. Where large industrial cities
now stand and concrete highways run, colonial visitors
found small farming villages surrounded by woodlands.

The state government situated in Trenton had yet to
come into existence, and New Jersey had two capitals, one
at Perth Amboy and the other at Burlington, these reflected

the time in the 17th century when it was two distinct colonies, East and West Jersey—what we would call today north and south New Jersey. Their society, their communities, their homes and day-to-day experiences were so different from our own.

Yet as different as it was, colonial New Jersey speaks to us today and shapes the lives of everyone who lives in the state and many who live beyond its borders. Then as now, the colony was home to a population that was ethnically and racially diverse. These people—such as English, Finns, and Scotch-Irish from western Europe, as well as Angolans and others from Africa—often living side by side, as they do today, were forced to accommodate and understand one another in order to live harmoniously.

New Jersey was an intellectual center, the only colony with two colleges (the College of New Jersey, later to become Princeton, and Queens, later to become Rutgers), which continue to play a vital role in the state today. And it was a spiritual center, home to some of the leading theologians in early America, whose values and beliefs still echo in American culture in the 21st century.

Early New Jersey society faced difficult problems and struggled to find peaceful solutions to them. When the colonists failed to do so, as they did in the 1660s, between

OPPOSITE: These pages from the journal of Annis Boudinot Stockton of New Brunswick, New Jersey, were written on May 22 1765, and contain a poem asking a friend to come visit.

1698 and 1701, again in the 1740s and 1750s, and finally in 1770, they turned to violence. Yet despite these failures, they managed to build a prosperous society.

I am pleased to act as a historical consultant for *Voices from Colonial America: New Jersey* because it introduces young readers to the complex and important issues raised by early New Jersey's history, providing necessary background information while examining the developments and problems that colonials faced on a human level. In so doing, the volume allows students to understand the influence of that past on their present lives, and to gain some understanding of how those who have preceded them in New Jersey wrestled with problems of change.

CHAPTER ONE

Colonial Beginnings

THE NATIVE LENNI-LENAPE PEOPLE *welcome Dutch and Swedish settlers to what is now New Jersey—but soon learn that life was better before the Europeans arrived.*

English explorer Henry Hudson arrived off the coast of northern New Jersey in 1609, but he hadn't come to stay. A group of merchants in the Netherlands had hired Hudson to find a quick water route from Europe to the spices and other riches that were available for sale in Asia. At this time, the only known ocean route from Europe to Asia was around the coast of Africa, and the trip could take several months to complete.

OPPOSITE: Henry Hudson first saw the New Jersey shoreline in 1609. His observations provided one of the first written descriptions of the area.

Hudson claimed the land around what is now known as the Hudson and Delaware Rivers for the Netherlands. This land, which the Dutch called New Netherland, included present-day New Jersey and New York.

Hudson's journey provided one of the first written descriptions of the New Jersey area. Robert Juet, a crewmember, kept a detailed journal throughout the trip. It is clear that Juet liked what he saw: *"This is a very good Land to fall with, and a pleasant Land to see."*

DUTCH SETTLEMENTS

Back home in the Netherlands, Juet's writings of forests filled with animals, streams stocked with fish, and fertile land intrigued the Dutch West India Company, a group of business leaders looking to make money. Dutch traders began to arrive in New Netherland in the early 1620s. They built trading posts along area waterways and bartered with the native people, exchanging European goods for the furs and hides of beavers and other animals.

The first Dutch settlement in New Jersey was Fort Nassau, in present-day Gloucester City. Founded in 1623, the fort was built along the Delaware River by Dutch explorer Cornelius Mey. The fort served as a trading center for the Dutch and the Indians. Within eight years, however, Fort Nassau's 24 occupants had all mysteriously disappeared, and the fort had fallen into disuse. Modern historians believe that the settlers may have just moved to a better trading location.

The Dutch West India Company realized that fur traders and merchants weren't enough to make the colony a success in the New World (as Europeans called the Americas). The company needed to find people willing to settle permanently in the area and make a living from farming. Farmers could provide food for themselves and other settlers there.

colony—a settlement that is controlled by a distant country

In 1629, the company began offering rewards to wealthy settlers known as patroons. To earn these rewards, the patroons had to foot the bill for their new settlements and promise to bring 50 adult colonists to New Netherland within four years. One reward was 16 miles (25 km) of river frontage anywhere except on Manhattan Island, in what is now New York. As a result, a few Dutch settled in what is present-day northern New Jersey.

patroon—a Dutch landowner in New Netherland

Many of these early farming communities failed because the patroons could not convince enough people to emigrate to the New World. Those who came resented the patroons for taking the best lands in the region. Many also resented having to work for the patroons for a certain number of years in exchange for farms of their own. In the coming years, only a handful of families lived in the part of New Netherland that would become known as New Jersey.

THE "ORIGINAL PEOPLE"

In the earliest days of Dutch settlement, the colonists lived side by side with the native peoples of the region. These tribes were members of a group known as the Lenni-Lenape. Lenni-Lenape is a Native American term for "original people." (Later, white settlers would call the tribe the Delaware, because they lived around the Delaware River.) Lenape people had lived in the area for thousands of years.

Lenape men used bows and arrows to hunt deer, bears, beavers, and ducks in the forests. They used nets of wild hemp, hooks of bone, and harpoons to catch shad, bass, sturgeon, oysters, and many other types of fish and shellfish in the rivers, streams, and ocean. The men were also in charge of making tools and hunting gear, as well as the canoes they used to travel from place to place.

Lenape women planted and tended crops: corn, beans, squash, and sweet potatoes. The women also gathered roots, nuts, and berries. They cared for the children, cooked the meals, wove mats, made pots out of clay, and made clothing, primarily from deerskin. Lenape women also took part in councils that made such major decisions as whether or not to go to war.

In the spring and summer, many Lenape people lived in farming villages. In the fall, however, they moved to temporary hunting camps. In 1628, Dutch colonist Isaack De Rasieres described the Lenapes' seasonal migration:

The grain being dried, they put it into baskets woven of rushes or wild hemp, and bury it in the earth, where they let it lie, and go with their husbands and children in October to hunt deer, leaving at home with their maize [corn] the old people who cannot follow; in December they return home and the flesh which they have not been able to eat while fresh, they smoke on the way, and bring it back with them.

This Lenape family was drawn by a Swedish settler in 1690.

FIRST CONTACT ?

THE FIRST EUROPEAN TO SET FOOT ON NEW JERSEY SOIL was probably Italian explorer Giovanni da Verrazano. Verrazano, sailing for France, explored the area in 1524. At this time, however, the French were not interested in creating a colony there. They, too, were looking for a water route to Asia.

Nearly 100 years before Henry Hudson arrived, Verrazano may have been the first European to come in contact with the Lenape people. He left behind a description of his meeting with the natives of the New Jersey region:

The people were about the same as we had met before [farther south]. They were dressed with bird feathers of different colors, and came toward us happily, giving loud shouts of admiration, and showed us where we could take the boat safely. We entered the river into the land for about half a league [1. 5 miles (2. 4 km)], where we saw that it formed a very beautiful lake . . . on which about thirty of their barks [boats] were going from one side to the other, carrying an infinite number of people coming from different parts to see us.

Robert Juet's journal describes one of the earliest encounters between the Lenape and Hudson's men in this area: *"This day the people of the Countrey came aboord of us, seeming very glad of our comming. . . . They desire Cloathes, and are very civill."* Problems soon arose, however. Two days later, one of Hudson's crew was killed by a Lenape arrow while out exploring. Juet did not explain why the man was attacked.

FROM FRIENDS TO FOES

At first, the Lenape were willing to share the land with the Dutch and even help the patroons and colonists survive. The Indians were very interested in the goods that the Dutch were offering to trade. The Dutch never saw the Indians as equals, however. Instead, they looked down upon the Indians, viewing them as children or savages that could be trained to behave like Europeans. In 1628, Johannes De Laet, a Dutch writer, wrote that the Lenape were *"well disposed, if they are only well treated . . . But with mild and proper treatment, and especially by [communication] with Christians, this people might be civilized and brought under better regulation."*

The Lenape introduced the settlers to corn, beans, and squash and taught them how to plant these vegetables in the same spot. First, the Lenape dug a hole and placed a dead fish inside to fertilize the ground. Next, corn was planted at the top of the mound. Once the cornstalks came up, beans and squash were planted in the mound. The beans used the cornstalks as poles to grow on. The squash plants took up space and prevented weeds from growing in the soil.

The Lenape also taught the settlers how to grind corn kernels to make cornmeal and how to store the corn and meal to make them last through the winter. Some Lenape even worked as servants in Dutch homes. The Lenape came to rely on the Dutch for a steady supply of European goods. They traded animal skins, vegetables, and help for such items as cooking tools, guns, and liquor.

Troubles between the two groups soon arose, however. Chief among these were a misunderstanding between the Dutch and the Lenape about land sales and Dutch mistreatment of the Native Americans. Conflicts with the Lenape would play a key role in preventing the Dutch from creating a successful colony in what is now New Jersey.

The Lenape people did not have the same concept of land ownership and sales as the Dutch did. When the Lenape accepted gifts from the Dutch, they believed that they were being paid for permission to live and hunt on the land. Because the Lenape believed that the land could not be owned, they expected that they, too, would continue using the same land. The Dutch had a very different understanding. They treated the land sales just as they did back home in Europe: Once they had purchased a parcel of land, it became entirely—and exclusively—theirs. The Lenape, in the Dutch view, no longer had any rights to use the land.

According to geographer Peter Wacker, 17th-century Europeans believed that *"Christians had not only the moral right but legal justification as well to spread their dominion over the Earth."* They looked down upon the Indians as people to be subdued and brought into the light of Christianity. This attitude was common from the earliest days of European exploration, especially amongst the Spanish and Portuguese.

In 1639, the governor of New Netherland began taxing the Lenape who lived on "Dutch" land. The Lenape could pay the tax with corn, furs, or wampum. The Indians were unhappy with the tax and refused to pay it. They saw no reason to pay for the use of land that belonged to everyone.

wampum—strings of dark purple and white beads made out of seashells that were used by some Native Americans as money; the Dutch used wampum to trade with the Lenape and other native tribes for animal furs and skins.

Relations between the Lenape and the Europeans worsened over the next four years. In 1643, the Dutch attacked a Lenape camp and killed about 80 natives. War broke out, and in about 18 months, the Lenape had destroyed farms, ruined crops, and driven nearly all the Dutch settlers across the Hudson River to Manhattan Island. The following spring, the Lenape and the Dutch made a peace agreement, and Dutch settlers soon began moving back across the Hudson.

In 1655, problems flared up between the Dutch and the Lenape once again. After a colonist shot a Lenape girl for stealing a peach from his orchard, native warriors attacked the settlement of Pavonia, which included nearly

30 farms. During the "Peach War," many settlers were killed, and Pavonia was nearly destroyed. Once again, the Dutch were driven across the river to Manhattan. For the next five years, most Dutch settlers would remain there. They would return to the west side of the Hudson only when Lenape populations dwindled because of disease, warfare with other tribes, and migration.

The most serious cause of the shrinking Native American population was European diseases. Epidemics of smallpox and other diseases from Europe, while dangerous to the colonists, proved devastating to native tribes who had no natural resistance to these illnesses. The first epidemic of smallpox spread quickly through the region in 1633, and others followed in later years. Many Lenape died in these epidemics, and the area's native population declined as the years wore on. Less than a hundred years after Hudson had visited the region, disease had taken a serious toll. In 1698, Englishman Gabriel Thomas wrote: *"The Dutch and Sweeds inform us that [the native people] are greatly decreased in number to what they were when they came first into this Country: And the Indians themselves say, that two of them die to every one Christian that comes in here."*

epidemic—the rapid spread of disease among many people

By 1750, as much as 90 percent of the Lenape population had been wiped out—mainly by disease. Some Lenape left the area, migrating to Pennsylvania and Ohio. Only a small number remained scattered throughout New Jersey.

NEW SWEDEN

The Dutch weren't the only Europeans interested in the area now known as New Jersey. In 1638, a company made up of Swedish and Dutch merchants hired Dutchman Peter Minuit to found a colony in the region. Like the Dutch West India Company, the New Sweden Company wanted to exploit the natural resources of the area. Their choice of Minuit was a smart one: Minuit, who had served as New Netherland's first governor, was well acquainted with the area. The Swedish government agreed to sponsor Minuit's new colony.

Minuit and his men sailed up the Delaware River and claimed the region for Sweden, naming it New Sweden. Minuit secured Sweden's claim to the region by purchasing the land from the Lenape. The center of the new colony was Fort Christina, on the west side of the river in what is now Wilmington, Delaware.

Peter Minuit settled the New Sweden colony after purchasing the land from the Lenni-Lenape.

Only a handful of New Sweden's settlers chose to make their homes on the east, or New Jersey, side of the river.

About half of the earliest settlers in New Sweden were Finns, many of whom had formerly lived in Sweden. The Finns were regarded as "undesirable" in Sweden because they burned forests before planting crops. Although this agricultural practice was common in other areas, the Swedes thought it was harmful to their forestland, so Swedish officials encouraged the Finns in Sweden to migrate to America.

The first Swedish settlement built in New Jersey was Fort Elfsborg, near present-day Salem, founded in 1643. Few people lived there, and it was abandoned in 1651.

Like the Dutch, the Swedes traded with the Native Americans for animal furs and skins. The Dutch, however, wanted no competition in their trade with local tribes. So the Dutch took every chance to make life difficult for the new arrivals. In a 1647 report, New Sweden's governor, Johan Printz, wrote, *"They destroy our trade everywhere. . . . They stir up the savages against us."*

Printz also had little use for the Lenape people. In a report, the governor wrote,

> *Nothing would be better than that a couple of hundred soldiers should be sent here and kept here until we broke the necks of all them [Lenape] in the river. . . . Then each one [Swede] could be secure here at his work, and feed and nourish himself unmolested without their maize, and also we could take possession of the places (which are the most fruitful) that the savages now possess.*

In return, the Lenape didn't think much of New Sweden's governor. They nicknamed Printz—who was 6 feet

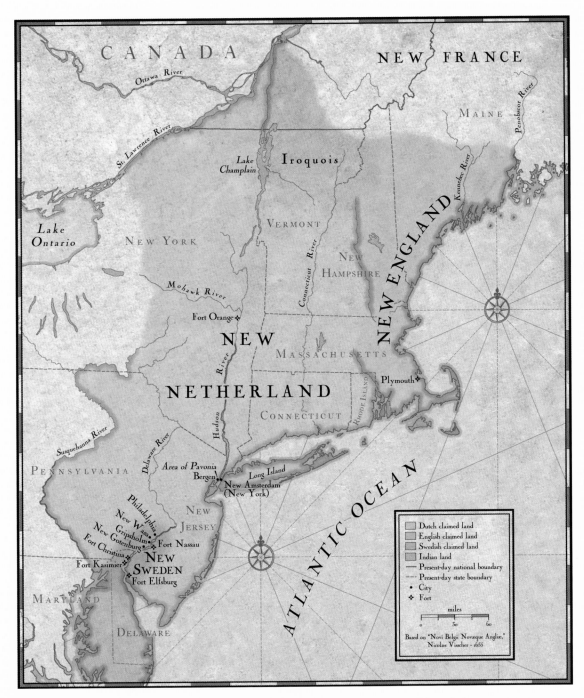

This map, based on maps of the early 1600s, gives an idea of the
boundaries of New Netherland and New Sweden as estimated today.

(1.8 m) tall and weighed 400 pounds (181 kg)—"Big Tub."

Finnish and Swedish settlers made an important contribution to colonial history. After arriving in the New World, they built log cabins similar to the ones they had lived in at home. Log cabins were quicker and easier to construct than houses made of smooth wooden boards. Finns and Swedes also brought from home a new tool, called an ax. They used the ax to clear land for settlement, cutting wood that could be used for building houses and burned for heating and cooking.

Johan Printz, governor of New Sweden, was unusually big and heavy for a man of his time. Printz had an unfriendly relationship with his Dutch neighbors in New Netherland and with the Lenni-Lenape who lived among New Sweden's settlers.

New Sweden did not prosper. A visitor to the area described it as a *"poor, sandy and abominable country."* By 1654, only about 360 people lived in the entire colony. Many colonists were close to starvation and ready to give up. In 1655, the Dutch conquered New Sweden. The area along the Delaware River once again became part of New Netherland. Although about 30 Swedish settlers returned to Sweden, the rest chose to remain and live under Dutch rule.

THE FIRST PERMANENT EUROPEAN TOWN

The center of life in the Dutch colony—and the most successful settlement—was New Amsterdam, located on the southern tip of Manhattan Island. New Amsterdam served as New Netherland's capital and chief trading center. Its fort also provided protection to colonists from other Dutch settlements during native attacks.

In 1661, more than 30 years after the founding of the first Dutch settlement, Tielman Van Vleck founded Bergen, at present-day Jersey City. Bergen, located between the Hackensack and Hudson Rivers, was the first permanent settlement in New Jersey.

Bergen's economy was based on agriculture. Farms were set up outside the town's walls. Inside the new town, a sawmill for cutting wood was quickly built. Other early buildings included a Dutch Reformed church, an elementary school, and a small fort called a blockhouse.

Bergen had its own government, led by a town leader called a *schout*. Bergen's first schout was Van Vleck himself. The settlement also had its own justice system. Court was held every two weeks, except at harvest time. The court tried such minor crimes as fighting, cursing, and drawing a weapon. People who committed more serious crimes, such as murder or theft, were sent to New Amsterdam for trial.

✕✕✕✕✕✕✕✕✕ P R O F I L E ✕✕✕✕✕✕✕✕✕

Tielman Van Vleck

T ielman Van Vleck, the founder of New Jersey's first permanent settlement, was born in Bremen, Germany, around 1614 and studied law in his native country. Arriving in New Netherland around 1658, Van Vleck petitioned the Dutch governor for permission to found a settlement near Pavonia. Although his first two petitions were denied, he was finally allowed to create a new town, named Bergen, the Dutch word for "hill."

After the English took control of New Jersey in 1664, Van Vleck, like most other Bergen citizens, took an oath of loyalty to the new government. He was named the town's clerk. Van Vleck spent the rest of his life in Bergen, helping the new settlement grow and thrive. He died around 1670.

LIFE IN THE EARLY SETTLEMENTS

During the mid-1600s, most early Dutch settlers in New Netherland were farmers. Upon arriving, their first task was to clear a space in the wilderness to live, but the average settler could clear no more than 2 acres (0.8 ha) a year. When they could, settlers built their homes on plots that had already been cleared by the Lenape. The settlers built farms called *bouweries*. These farms were often miles away from one another, so Dutch families had to learn to survive on their own.

bouweries—small Dutch farms in New Netherland

Corn was the most important crop for Dutch settlers. They ate the kernels, fed the stalks to livestock, and stuffed their mattresses with corn husks. Corn cobs were used to seal jugs or as pipes.

Some of the first Dutch homes were temporary sod houses. Settlers built a sod house by digging a large cellar. Then they placed timber along the walls and arranged wood planks over the dirt floor. Branches covered with grass and sod formed a roof. Some settlers lived in these sod homes for up to four years until they could construct new, more permanent wooden houses.

Early Dutch wooden houses were not very comfortable. One European visitor to a drafty New Jersey home in 1679 described it as *"wretchedly constructed."* He complained that the only way to keep warm was to sit *"so close to the fire as almost to burn yourself."* The traveler spoke more kindly of Swedish log cabins, calling them *"tight and warm."*

Early settlers in New Jersey spoke Dutch, used Dutch money, and practiced Dutch customs. But Dutch dominance of New Jersey was about to come to a close. The British wanted to control the entire Atlantic coast, and a few struggling Dutch and Swedish settlements were not going to stop them. ❈

CHAPTER TWO

An English Colony

THE ENGLISH TAKE CONTROL, *turning a struggling section of New Netherland into the growing colony of New Jersey.*

he Dutch and Swedes were not the only Europeans who wanted to own the New Jersey region. The English claimed that John Cabot's 1497 explorations of the region that would become known as New England gave them the rights to all the land along North America's east coast. (New England is a region that includes present-day Maine, New Hampshire, Vermont, Massachusetts, Rhode Island, and Connecticut.) New Netherland was the only non-British settlement in the region. The English wanted the entire area for their own.

OPPOSITE: King Charles II of England took New Netherland from the Dutch in an effort to bring the entire East Coast under British control.

They also wanted to take control of the Dutch fur trade in New Netherland.

John Cabot is shown here in 1497
off the coast of North America.

In 1664, King Charles II of England decided to take New Netherland from the Dutch. In March, Charles granted all the land between the Connecticut and Delaware Rivers to his brother James, Duke of York and Albany. This meant that, according to the English, the Duke of York now owned the areas that are known today as New Jersey, New York, and Delaware, and parts of New England.

In September 1664, four English warships landed off New Amsterdam. English colonel Richard Nicolls ordered

Dutch governor Peter Stuyvesant to surrender. Knowing that his small group of settlers could never defend the colony, Stuyvesant agreed. New Netherland ceased to exist, New Amsterdam was renamed New York, and present-day New Jersey became known as New Albania.

Soon after he sent Nicolls to conquer and govern New Netherland, the Duke of York gave away the region of New Albania, between the Hudson and Delaware Rivers, to his two friends, Lord John Berkeley and Sir George Carteret. The grant allowed the two men to act as proprietors of the land. The duke even renamed the land "New Jersey" in honor of Sir George's birthplace on the island of Jersey. Both Carteret and Berkeley believed that the grant also allowed them to govern their land. Neither man, however, chose to move to his new property. News of the duke's gift to his two favorites did not reach Nicolls in New York. In New Jersey, Nicolls found a small, struggling colony with just a few Dutch settlements. He knew he needed to attract more settlers. Nicolls's first move was to allow the Dutch settlers to remain—as long as they swore allegiance to the king of England. The Dutch were allowed the same rights and privileges as English settlers. For example, they chose their own town officials, created their own laws, and enjoyed freedom of worship. The surrender agreement between the English and the Dutch said that the Dutch colonists *"shall continue free [citizens], and shall*

proprietor—one of the early owners of colonial land in New Jersey

enjoy their lands, houses and goods, wheresoever they are within this country, and dispose of them as they please. The Dutch here shall enjoy their own customs concerning their inheritances." Under English rule, Dutch life continued as usual.

Next, Nicolls encouraged English colonists on more crowded Long Island to move to New Albania. Long Island is a large island located just southeast of Manhattan Island. With Nicolls's blessing, a group of Puritans from Long Island bought a piece of land in New Jersey from the Lenape in late 1664. The Puritans thought that buying the land would solidify their own claims to it. Their new land was located just across New York Bay

Puritans—Protestants who believed in strict morals and simple forms of worship

from Long Island. In exchange for the land, the Puritans paid the Lenape some cloth, "two made Coats, two Guns, two Kettles, Ten barrs of Lead, Twenty Handfuls of Powder," and some wampum. The total value of the goods was equal to about $3,300 in today's dollars. Soon, the colonists from Long Island began building the settlement that would become Elizabethtown.

Elizabethtown's first colonists were farmers, but the town's site was also perfect for trade. It was close to New York and had easy access to the Atlantic Ocean. Other English settlements in New Jersey, including Newark, Middletown, and Shrewsbury, soon followed.

The Lenape were, at first, helpful to the new arrivals. They hoped to be treated better by the English settlers than they had been by the Dutch. They traded with the colonists, supplying them with food, furs, and deerskins. Later, however, the Lenape learned that the English had the same ideas about land ownership that the Dutch had. Most English settlers, especially those in the eastern part of the colony, also treated the Lenape as inferior beings.

THE PROPRIETORS GET INVOLVED

In 1665, Lord John Berkeley and Sir George Carteret decided to send their own governor to take control of New Jersey. Philip Carteret, a distant cousin of Sir George, arrived in the colony in July 1665. He brought with him about 30 settlers from England's Isle of Jersey. The settlers had been promised large chunks of land in exchange for founding new towns.

Preparing for a NEW HOME

A NUMBER OF NEW JERSEY'S settlers came from England, Scotland, and Ireland. Many of these early settlers from Europe were Quakers seeking freedom of religion or indentured servants hoping for a better life. They must have wondered what to bring with them to the New World. In 1682, a pamphlet about the colony solved this problem with the following short list: *"The goods to be carried there, are, first, for people's own use, all sorts of apparel and household stuff, and also utensils for husbandry and building: secondly, linnen and woollen cloths and stuffs, fitting for apparel . . . and which are fit for [sale] in the country."*

Governor Carteret also brought with him a special document from proprietors Carteret and Berkeley. Called the Concessions and Agreements, the document would serve as a charter for the new colony. New Jersey's charter was written to encourage settlement. The Concessions and Agreements promised freedom of religion and free land to *"all such as shall settle and plant [in New Jersey]."* The promise of religious freedom was very attractive to Quakers and other Protestants who were being persecuted throughout Europe at this time. The promise of free land was appealing to people with little money, who would not normally be able to afford their own homes and farms.

charter— a written document that grants a colony certain rights and privileges, including the right to exist

Quakers—members of a Protestant religious group called the Society of Friends; Quakers opposed war and taking oaths and held simple religious services

Elizabethtown's colonists were surprised by Governor Carteret's arrival. They were shocked to hear that they no longer owned the land they lived on—even though they had purchased it from the Lenape with Governor Nicolls's approval. According to Carteret, Nicolls did not have the authority to allow the settlers to purchase land owned by the proprietors. The colonists were also upset when Carteret announced that, beginning in 1670, all eastern New Jersey colonists would have to pay a tax on the lands they no longer owned. This tax was known as a *quitrent*. (Dutch settlers in Bergen and some other places were exempted from the quitrent under Carteret's charter.) Carteret had set in motion a conflict over land ownership that would rage until the beginning of the American Revolution.

Most early colonists in New Jersey made their living by farming.

GOVERNMENT AND LAW IN EARLY NEW JERSEY

The first formal government of the British colony of New Jersey, called the General Assembly, was laid out in the Concessions and Agreements. The head of the colonial government was the governor, who was chosen by the proprietors. To assist in running the colony, the governor

General Assembly— the New Jersey colony's lawmaking body

could choose a council of as many as 12 residents. In addition to the governor and the council, the General Assembly included a group of 12 colonists known as deputies. The deputies were elected each year by the freemen (adult males who were not indentured servants or slaves) of New Jersey.

indentured servant—a person who agreed to work for a certain period of time, usually six years, in exchange for paid passage to a colony

In May 1668, New Jersey's General Assembly met for the first time in Elizabethtown, the colony's capital. During the five-day session, officials created the colony's first code of laws. These first laws were very severe, showing the strong influence of the Puritan settlers who had come to the colony over the past few years. The Puritans made sure that many of the colony's early laws were based upon the Bible.

The code of laws set out punishments for crimes ranging from murder to *"the beastly vice"* of drunkenness. Penalties included whipping, banishment, and sitting in the public stocks. There was also a colonial law under which a person who committed burglary or robbery for a third time was eligible for the death penalty.

stocks—wooden frames with holes for the legs and arms; used as a form of public punishment

Other early New Jersey laws were created to protect the young colony from outside enemies, including Native Americans tribes or foreign invaders. One law required all males between the ages of 16 and 60 to own arms and ammunition. In addition, every town had to have a fortress for the defense of women, children, ammunition, and food. Colonists were forbidden to sell guns or ammunition to the Indians.

Many laws dealt with the well-being of New Jersey's colonists. One law, for example, offered 15 shillings (about $125 in today's money) for each wolf that was killed in the colony. Another ordered that all leather, beef, and pork made in New Jersey be inspected. There was even a law against gossip: Anyone who spread false news was fined ten shillings (about $80 in today's money).

A number of New Jersey laws were aimed at preventing or fighting fires. Fires were a common occurrence in colonial times. Most structures were made of wood, and open fires inside homes were used for cooking and heating. In Elizabethtown, families had to own a ladder and pail for firefighting. They also had to clean their chimneys once a month during the winter.

Although the General Assembly made laws for the whole colony, Elizabethtown and other English settlements also had their own governments. Each town held meetings where freemen had the chance to speak out and vote on issues that affected them. Town officials were elected at these meetings. Elected officials included a town clerk, tax collector, town watchman, branding master (someone who branded cattle and other livestock), and fence viewer (someone who inspected each colonist's fences to make sure they were well-built and secure).

NATIVE PESTS

WOLVES AND OTHER WILD ANIMALS WEREN'T THE ONLY PESTS faced by New Jersey's colonists. Mosquitoes were a real nuisance, especially in swampy or wet areas. In a time without bug zappers, insect repellant, or screens for windows and doors, Swedish settlers started the practice of lighting bonfires in front of their homes to drive the flying menaces away. The bugs were so bad that Peter Kalm, who lived in the colony from 1748 to 1751, took the time to write about them:

In daytime or at night they come into the houses, and when people have gone to bed they begin their disagreeable humming approach nearer and nearer to the bed, and at last suck up so much blood that they can hardly fly away. . . . When they stung me here at night, my face was so disfigured by little red spots and blisters that I was almost ashamed to show myself.

A GROWING COLONY

In the 1660s, word quickly spread about the good, fertile land to be had in New Jersey. The best lands for settlement were along the Hudson and Delaware Rivers, where the first settlers—Dutch, Swedes, Finns, and English—made their homes. Later colonists built houses along the smaller rivers and streams in the center of the colony. These waterways connected the new settlers to the larger towns, allowing people and goods to be transported from one place to another. The last section of the colony to be settled was the mountainous northwest.

New Jersey's temperate climate was also a draw for many settlers. Winters in New Jersey were not nearly as cold as those in New England, while the summers were not nearly as hot as those in the colonies to the south. In 1698, colonist Gabriel Thomas wrote an account of West Jersey. *"The Air is very Clear, Sweet and Wholesome,"* he wrote. *"In the depth of Winter it is something colder, but as much hotter in the heighth of Summer than in England."* His was just one of many written accounts that were intended to entice new settlers to come to New Jersey.

EARLY ECONOMY

Like the Dutch before them, New Jersey's early English settlers relied on the colony's natural resources of fertile land, fish-stocked waters, and vast forests. The three most important industries in the mid-1600s were farming, fishing, and lumber. Excessive trapping had already ended the importance of the fur trade to New Jersey's economy by nearly wiping out the supply of fur-bearing animals in the area.

Wheat was the colony's major crop, followed by corn and hay. By the mid-1700s, New Jersey was one of the "bread colonies" that provided such grains as wheat and rye to the other British colonies in America. Colonial farmers also raised pigs, cattle, chickens, goats, and horses. Pigs were the most important animals in the early colony, and New Jersey settlers of the time ate more pork than any other meat. On the eve of the American Revolution, New Jersey was the top sheep-raising colony, with 144,000 sheep.

At first, pigs and other livestock were allowed to roam free. As the livestock population grew, however, the animals began causing damage to neighboring land. Throughout the colonial period, a number of laws were created to address the problem. A 1704 law, for example, stated that *"any person or persons that shall find any Swine trespassing upon his or their Land, may forth-with kill such Swine, and keep them to his or their own proper use."*

In the spring, farm families plowed and planted. In the summer, they harvested their crops. In the fall, some farmers sowed winter wheat, to be harvested in the spring. Even the winter was a time of activity. The farm family slaughtered livestock, threshed grain, and did indoor and outdoor chores that they couldn't get to during the rest of the year. The family sold or traded extra grain to buy food and other supplies.

thresh—to beat wheat to remove the grain from the plant

Fishing was also important, especially along the major rivers and the Atlantic coast. Shad, bass, and sturgeon were just a few of the fish taken from Jersey waters. New Jersey oysters were a colonial treat. Wealthy merchants, landowners, and lawyers who lived inland had oysters shipped to them from the coast.

Wood was highly valued in England and in other British colonies for shipbuilding and home construction. The most prized wood was white cedar. Oak and pine were also cut. As people in New York City and Philadelphia, Pennsylvania, used up their timber, they turned to New Jersey for a constant supply of wood. As a result, the best wood in New Jersey's central forests had all been cut by the 1760s.

Under English control, New Jersey began to grow and thrive. People traveled from Europe and other colonies to make new homes there and the economy slowly developed. Problems between Jersey's new settlers and the proprietors, however, would soon cause a serious split in the colony. 🞓

A sawmill for cutting wood, like the one shown here, was usually one of the first structures to be built in an early New Jersey town.

The People of New Jersey

NEW JERSEY'S PROMISE *of religious freedom and self-government attracts a wide variety of people, even as the colony splits into two very different sections.*

s the years passed, New Jersey developed into one of the most ethnically diverse of all the Colonies. People from the Netherlands, Sweden, Finland, England, Scotland, Ireland, Germany, and France were attracted to New Jersey by the promise of religious freedom and available land. They brought with them their own languages, religions, cultures, habits, and beliefs.

The 1670s were a time of turmoil for New Jersey. Many of the colony's settlers refused to pay the quitrent

OPPOSITE: This woodcut illustrates the First Burlington Meetinghouse, which was the center of the Quaker community in New Jersey in the late 1600s. Quakers would gather there for worship, town meetings, and social occasions.

imposed upon them in 1670 by the proprietors. Some colonists were so upset that in 1672, they formed a rebel assembly that met without Governor Philip Carteret's knowledge. This assembly appointed its own governor to replace Carteret. It would take two years before Carteret was restored as governor.

In 1674, Proprietor Berkeley, now in need of money, sold his rights in New Jersey to two English Quakers, John Fenwick and Edward Byllynge. Quakers were members of a religious group that called themselves the Society of Friends. They were a peace-loving people who believed in the goodness of humanity and were against taking part in wars or swearing oaths. The Quakers did not have priests or ministers, and they did not follow any ceremonies or rituals during worship

Lord John Berkeley sold his rights in New Jersey to Quakers John Fenwick and Edward Byllynge.

services. They worshipped in silence, unless an individual was moved by the Holy Spirit to speak. In Europe, these unusual religious practices made the Quakers targets of ridicule and persecution. The Quakers who bought Berkeley's interest in New Jersey were attracted by the colony's promise of freedom of worship.

After the sale, King Charles II gave Proprietor Carteret sole control of the eastern section of the colony, while Fenwick and Byllynge were given control of the west. In 1676, the king signed the Quintipartite Deed to formally separate the colony into East New Jersey and West New Jersey. The boundary between the two colonies ran from High Point, a mountain in the north, to Little Egg Harbor, on the colony's southeastern coast. The two new colonies were more different than alike.

William Penn
& NEW JERSEY

A BANKRUPT EDWARD BYLLYNGE PLACED HIS INTEREST in West New Jersey in trust with William Penn and several other men in 1676. Penn was a Quaker who believed that the new colony would provide a safe haven for persecuted Quakers. In August 1677, he and more than 200 other Quakers arrived in West New Jersey on board the ship *Kent* out of London. Once in the colony, Penn settled in the town of Salem, where he established an estate with more than 12,000 acres (4,900 ha). As a colonial leader, he signed the new colony's constitution.

In 1680, Sir George Carteret died. Two years later, Penn and several other men bought the rights to East New Jersey. That same year, however, Penn decided to found a new colony to the west of New Jersey that would become known as Pennsylvania. Just a few months after obtaining rights to East New Jersey, he transferred his interests in the two Jerseys to other Quakers.

WEST NEW JERSEY

The Quakers in control of West New Jersey set out to create a colony where all people could live together peacefully. The colony's Concessions, written in 1677, promised an assembly elected by the colonists, as well as freedom of religion to all who settled there. The Quaker document was meant to serve as a *"foundation for after ages [generations to come] to understand their liberty as men and christians."*

Many Quaker families from England, Ireland, and Wales emigrated to West New Jersey. Instead of settling in towns, they most often spread out, clearing land for farms throughout the countryside. By the late 1600s, about 3,500 people—most of them Quakers—lived in West New Jersey. Settlement in West New Jersey was heaviest along the Delaware River, where major towns included Salem, Greenwich, and Burlington. Founded in 1678, Burlington served as West New Jersey's capital.

In 1682, William Penn founded Philadelphia on the Pennsylvania side of the Delaware. The site was a good one, with easy access to the Atlantic Ocean. As the city grew and prospered, it became an important trade center for the West New Jersey colonists. By the early 1700s, all goods produced in

Quaker men often wore large hats, which they refused to take off to anyone but God at anytime except during prayer.

the colony—cloth, wheat, livestock, fish, shell-fish, and wood—passed through Penn's city before being shipped to other places. Goods from around the world—furniture, clothing, farming equipment, and household items—passed first through Philadelphia before being sent on for sale in West New Jersey.

EAST NEW JERSEY

In 1682, William Penn and 11 other Quakers bought the rights to East New Jersey from Sir George Carteret's widow. The 12 men then took on 12 partners, both Quakers and Scottish Presbyterians. By the end of the year, the Quaker proprietors—especially William Penn—had turned their attention to Pennsylvania, leaving the Scottish proprietors in charge of East New Jersey. The Scottish proprietors worked hard to attract new settlers to their colony. They published pamphlets—some more fiction than fact—that described the beauty and potential of the colony.

Like men's clothing, Quaker women's wear was simple in design, dark in color, and modestly cut, but a woman's dress might be made of a rich material.

Many of the pamphlets and letters sent to Europe focused on—and greatly exaggerated—the colony's healthful qualities. In 1685, for example, Charles Gordon, a colonist living in the town of Woodbridge (settled in 1664), wrote to a friend in Scotland that he was

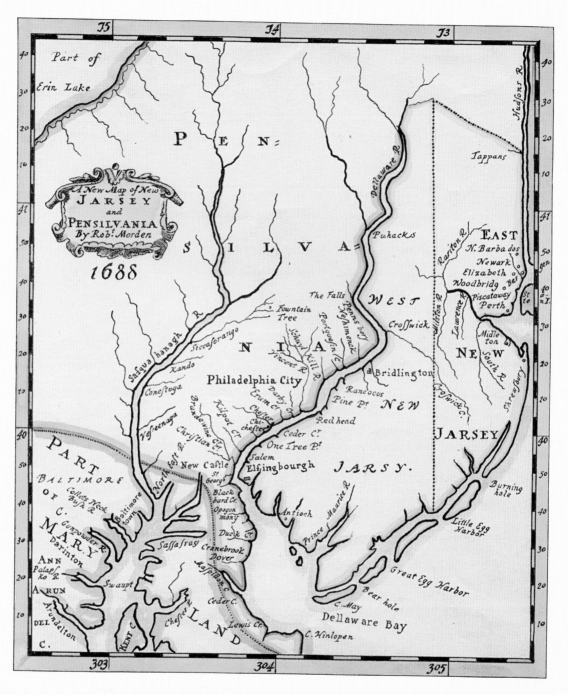

The boundary between East and West Jersey ran from High Point in the
northern mountains to Little Egg Harbor along the shore.

"not troubled with coughs and head aikes . . . which is likewise a great motive for me to stay in this Countrey." He wrote to his brother, a physician, the same year, "If you design to come hither yourself, you may come as a planter; or as a merchant, or as a doctor of medicine. I cannot advise you, as I can hear of no diseases here to cure, but some Agues, and some cutted fingers and legs."

In a 1682 letter to his bosses in London, East New Jersey's deputy governor, Thomas Rudyard, described the people and conditions in the colony: "The people are generally a sober professing people, wise in their generation, courteous in their behavior and respectful to us in office among them . . . there is not an industrious man, but by God's blessing, may not only have a comfortable but plentiful supply of all things necessary for this life."

As a result of the proprietors' efforts, East New Jersey grew quickly. Many of the new arrivals were immigrants from Scotland who hoped to find a better life in East New Jersey. Land here was cheaper than in Scotland, and there were more chances for young people to make a good living and start families. Many of the Scottish settlers arrived as indentured servants. An indentured servant agreed to work for a certain period of time in exchange for paid passage to the Colonies. After the period of service was over, the servant was usually given a piece of land and some supplies.

Other settlers migrated from other British colonies in America, particularly Connecticut and New York. Many of these migrants were Puritans who were unhappy with the relaxation of religious laws and beliefs in their former homes.

They hoped to found towns where they could more faithfully follow their strict religious beliefs. Scotch-Irish settlers came from Ireland and Germans came from Germany. Many settlers were poor and hoped that a move to the New World would bring them new economic opportunities. Others chose New Jersey for its guarantee of religious freedom.

Scotch-Irish—Scottish people who had settled in Northern Ireland for a time before migrating to America

The Scottish proprietors founded Perth Amboy on the Raritan River. The new settlement became East New Jersey's capital and an important port. In 1684, John Reid wrote a letter about the virtues of the new settlement. He said, *"It is one of the best places in America, by the report of all Travellers. For a town of trade, for my part, I never saw any so conveniently seated."*

Although East New Jersey grew more rapidly than its sister colony, it was still a very wild and wooded area. One traveler, making his way to New York from East New Jersey, got quite lost, despite having an Indian guide. He wrote in his journal, *"We travelled that day and saw no tame creature, at night we kindled a fire in the wilderness and lay by it."*

East New Jersey looked to New York City for supplies and trade. At first, most contact between the two colonies was by water. Ships from New York brought merchandise into Perth Amboy, and from there, the goods were transported to other East New Jersey settlements. Wheat, pork, and beef from East New Jersey were

TALL
Reptile
Tales

COLONISTS FROM SCOTLAND AND England had never before seen rattlesnakes. A number of interesting tales about the reptiles arose, as shown in a 1685 letter from Scottish settler James Johnston to a friend back home:

You cannot come nigh a rattle-Snake, but they will rattle with their taile, whereby a man is advertised either to kill them, or go by them; they frequently charm Squirrels, or other little Beasts off the tops of the Trees unto their mouth, and that without touching them with their teeth; which if they did, they would poison themselves.

shipped from Perth Amboy to New York City before moving on to other ports. In the late 1600s and early 1700s, East New Jersey would try to bypass New York by building ports and starting its own shipping businesses.

Splitting New Jersey into two separate colonies had little effect on solving the many problems the early settlers faced. Some of the most pressing issues—taxation debates and land rights disputes—would continue to plague settlers in both of the Jerseys throughout the colonial period. In the end, England would be forced to take a more active role in resolving the Jerseys' problems.

CHAPTER FOUR

Life in Royal New Jersey

EAST NEW JERSEY AND WEST NEW JERSEY reunite as the royal colony of New Jersey, while life for the colonists continues as normal.

B y the end of the 1690s, taxation and land rights disputes in both the New Jerseys were heating up once again. Many settlers in East New Jersey, especially those who had purchased their land from the Lenape or who had arrived before 1665, refused to pay the taxes imposed on them by the proprietors. In West New Jersey, settlers wanted the right to choose their own governor, someone who would protect land ownership rights and freedom of religion.

OPPOSITE: This woodcut from the 1600s shows boys participating in sports typical of those played by English boys in New Jersey at that time.

In 1700, colonists in some East New Jersey towns rioted, disrupted court sessions, and attacked public officials. In West New Jersey, a mob forced local officials into hiding after the proprietors announced a new tax.

Tired of all the trouble, the proprietors of both colonies agreed to turn their governing rights over to the English government. In 1702, Queen Anne combined both colonies into one New Jersey. The colony would be run by the royal governor of New York. Two capitals were selected for the colony: Burlington in the west and Perth Amboy in the east. The colonial assembly would take turns meeting in Burlington one year and then Perth Amboy the following year.

For the next 36 years, New Jersey would remain in New York's shadow. The shared governor's top priority was always the much larger New York, so that colony's interests were always placed above New Jersey's. Under less scrutiny than their neighbors to the north, however, New Jersey colonists enjoyed more local self-government than colonists elsewhere.

COLONIAL LIVING

In the early 1700s, most New Jersey families still relied on farming to make a living. Nearly everything a farming family needed could be grown or made at home.

Spinning wheel

Each family had a kitchen garden near the house where women grew vegetables and herbs. Most families also had an orchard with fruit trees.

Every colonial family kept a musket and gunpowder. The settlers hunted for meat and also had to protect their homes and crops from wild animals. Raccoons, squirrels, and crows ate the corn and other vegetables. Wolves and other predators preyed on livestock. Up until the mid-1700s, wild animals were plentiful. *"There were excessive numbers of wolves . . . and their howling and yelping might be heard all night,"* noted one Swedish settler.

HOUSING

In New Jersey's English settlements, the earliest permanent homes were small one-story houses made of planks held together by wooden pegs and roofed with thatch, or straw. Most homeowners started with one big room that was used for sleeping, eating, and all other household activities. They often added rooms later.

In the early 1700s, Dutch colonists had their own special style of housing, known today as Dutch colonial. Like the English, the Dutch imitated building styles from back home. A Dutch home at this time was made out of brick or stone, with a gambrel, or barn-like, roof.

Inside colonial houses, walls were covered with a type of plaster made out of clay and ground seashells. The low ceilings and small windows helped early colonists conserve heat, especially during the cold winter months. In some homes, an extra half-story, or loft, was used as an additional bedroom. This extra space could prove useful: as many as a dozen people might share one small house.

The Dutch colonial style of architecture, illustrated by this 1699 wood engraving of a New York house, is seen in homes in and around New Jersey today.

A huge, central fireplace was the most important feature of any Jersey home. A fire roared almost constantly, warming the house in the winter and serving as a year-round stove and oven. In front of the fire, the family cooked, ate, talked, and slept during cold nights. The need for firewood was constant, and the entire family pitched in to get wood. Firewood was a highly valued commodity, and as early as 1666, the colony passed laws that prevented people from chopping wood on land that was not their own.

In the early 1700s, most colonists did not have a lot of furniture. Instead of beds, many colonists used bedrolls called shakedowns. The shakedowns could be rolled up and tucked away during the day. Later, families might buy trundle beds. A trundle bed was a low, small bed that could be stored underneath a larger bed. Mattresses were stuffed with cornhusks or rags. A family might also own a chest or two for storing clothing and other items.

At dinnertime, colonists sat on stools or benches in front of a long board supported by trestles. A family ate from plates and bowls made out of wood. They used spoons and knives, but not forks. Forks didn't become popular in the United States until the early 1800s. Instead, colonists used their fingers as needed.

trestle—a wooden support used for holding up tables and other items

In addition to a musket, a family needed a hoe, a saw, and an ax. Some families also had spinning wheels to make yarn and thread from wool.

WORKING IN NEW JERSEY

As New Jersey grew in population, the demand for tradesmen also grew. In a 1684 letter, Scottish settler John Reid listed workers who would find easy employment in the colony. *"I know nothing wanting here, except that good Tradesmen*

. . . *are scarce," he wrote. "Smiths, Carpenters, Masons, Weavers, Taylors, Shoemakers, are very acceptable."* Mill workers of all types were also important and much needed in colonial New Jersey.

Tanning was an important occupation in New Jersey. Tanners made leather for boots, shoes, belts, and saddles. Elizabethtown was one of the major tanning centers.

tanning—the process of treating animal hides with a substance called tannin to turn them into leather

A more unusual job was that of the reeve. The reeves rounded up cows or pigs that had escaped from their owners. The runaway animals were taken to the village pound, where they could be picked up, for a fee, by their owners.

A WOMAN'S ROLE

A colonial wife was in charge of the home and everything in it. She supervised sewing, spinning, weaving, candle-making, cooking, cleaning, and preserving foods. She tended the kitchen garden and the family's orchard. In a farming family, women were also expected to help out on the farm.

One of the most important roles of colonial women was caring for the children. Because many early colonial families were large, this task could be exhausting. Esther Edwards Burr, a resident of Elizabethtown, wrote to a friend after the birth of her second child, Aaron, "*When I* had but one Child my hands were tied," she wrote, "but now I am tied hand and foot. (How I shall get along when I have got 1/2 dzn. or 10 Children I cant devise.)" Aaron Burr would grow up to serve under President Thomas Jefferson as the third vice president of the United States.

Colonial women had the exhausting task of managing everything in their homes in addition to caring for their often large families. A hardworking, loyal wife was considered an asset to her husband.

In New Jersey, women were expected to stay out of public affairs. Not all women agreed with this idea. Esther Burr wrote in a letter to her friend Sarah Prince of Boston,

> The Men say . . . that Women have no business to concern themselves about [public affairs] but trust to those that know better. . . . Indeed if I was convinced that our great men did act as they realy thought was for the Glory of God and the good of the Country it would go a great ways to meke me easy.

All of a New Jersey woman's property and money became her husband's after marriage. Her children officially belonged to her husband. New Jersey women could inherit land and property upon their husbands' deaths, however.

For women living in New Jersey and other colonies, a divorce was almost impossible to obtain. It could only be granted during a special meeting of the colonial assembly. For most women, escaping a troubled marriage meant running away and leaving their children behind.

CHILDREN

Most New Jersey families were quite large, with between seven and ten children. Children were important helpers around the home and on the farm. From the age of three, sons and daughters were expected to perform chores such as feeding chickens or weeding the kitchen garden. Later, they would help plant, tend, and harvest crops on the farm.

From the age of 12, both boys and girls might be apprenticed to tradesmen or other families to learn skills that would help them later in life. Boys, might work with blacksmiths or tanners to gain firsthand experience. Girls might be apprenticed to neighbors to better learn such domestic skills as baking, sewing, and spinning. Most apprentices received little or no pay while they learned a trade. Many were given food, clothing, and a place to sleep, however.

Once they were old enough, many young men left New Jersey and moved to the big cities of New York and Philadelphia. Most were attracted by the better jobs and social opportunities to be found in the larger cities. There, they could meet a large variety of people, perhaps apprentice with one of the city's artisans, or sign on for an ocean voyage down at the docks.

The Obligations of a PURITAN WIFE

THE FOLLOWING PIECE, WRITTEN by Benjamin Wadsworth in 1712, illustrates what was expected of Puritan wives—and most other colonial wives, for that matter—by their husbands.

Wives are part of the House and Family, and ought to be under the Husband's Government: they should Obey their own Husbands. . . . Yea, though possibly thou hast greater abilities of mind than he has, wast of some high birth, and he of a more mean Extract . . . yet since he is thy Husband, God has made him thy Head, and set him above thee, and made it thy duty to love and reverence him.

ILLNESS AND MEDICAL CARE

Sickness was cause for serious alarm during this period and epidemics were not uncommon. In the early 1700s, the most feared diseases were smallpox, the "bloody flux" (dysentery), and "putrid fever" (typhus). All these diseases were contagious, and each could prove deadly.

At the beginning of the 18th century, there were no schools of medicine anywhere in the Colonies. As a result, those few men who did practice medicine had very little formal training. Most colonial doctors got their knowledge of medicine by apprenticing with an older doctor for a while before striking out on their own. The success rate of these doctors was usually quite poor, and they were often looked down upon by other colonists.

Colonial doctors often did not have much formal training and could do little to prevent sickness or early death.

With few doctors, most colonists had to fend for themselves during times of illness. Housewives used herbal medicines made out of local plants such as Saint-John's-wort. Other colonial medicines were made up of parts from toads, snakes, and other animals. In colonial times, anyone could throw some ingredients into a bottle and call it a medicine. Some of these "cures" might make a patient sicker than before. Usually, staying healthy depended upon good genes and a bit of luck.

Each time a colonist became ill, friends and family worried that the sickness would kill the patient and spread to the rest of the community. In August 1755, Esther Burr's husband became ill. Although he soon recovered, his wife recounted her fear for his health to a friend:

> I watched with Mr. Burr last Night, and a most dreadfull night he had—he took a Vomit yesterday P.M. and it had the strangest effect on him that I ever saw in my Life. I expected for half an hour every minute he would die . . . this is sertain that if he han't spedy help he can't live long. . . .

The first to die were usually the very young and the very old. From July 23, 1776, to the end of October, Jemima Condict, of Morristown, New Jersey, recorded the deaths of more than 50 neighbors during an epidemic of the bloody flux. More than half of those who died were children. These terrible epidemics gave Condict and other colonists a less-than-hopeful view of life and death. In her journal, Condict recorded a poem: "Both few and evil are the days of man, / They quick away do pass." Although New Jersey's death rate was not as high as that of some other colonies, illness and premature death still touched nearly all families there. 🏵

CHAPTER FIVE

Servants and Slaves in New Jersey

Indentured servants, redemptioners, and slaves play an important role in the colony's growth and development.

 ome of the people who helped build the colony of New Jersey were indentured servants and redemptioners, brought to New Jersey with the promise that years of servitude would earn them freedom. Others were slaves, bought in Africa and then sold to slaveholders in the West Indies or the British Colonies in America. Native Americans were enslaved, too, although

OPPOSITE: This 18th-century engraving shows an American dyer being helped by indentured servants.

this was not as common in New Jersey as in some other colonies. Some Indians were captured by European settlers; others were sold to the settlers by enemy tribes that had captured them during tribal wars. All these people had little choice but to serve and obey the men and women to whom they were sold. Not only were slaves in bondage for life, but any children they had were automatically slaves, too.

Slaves from Africa were sometimes sold to owners in New Jersey.

INDENTURED SERVANTS AND REDEMPTIONERS

Some of the settlers who came to New Jersey from Europe were indentured servants. Although the amount of time that a worker was bound to serve varied, the average period was six years. Most indentured servants in New Jersey were Scotch-Irish or German. Others were French, Swiss, or Scottish.

Other colonists came to New Jersey as redemptioners. On arrival, redemptioners owed the ship's captain the cost of the trip, so they tried to sell their services for a certain period of time to the highest bidder. If no one hired a new arrival, the ship's captain could sell

redemptioner—a person who came to America without the money to pay for the passage

him or her as a servant to anyone on any terms. It was not unusual to see a captain trying to sell large groups of immigrants in the New Jersey countryside. These captains earned the nickname "soul-drivers."

In New Jersey, indentured servants and redemptioners performed any tasks assigned to them. Many farmed, but others worked in iron factories or in whaling, ship-building, or other industries. For some, it was the chance to learn a valuable trade that would allow them to earn a good living once their service was over. In an effort to convince more people from Scotland to migrate to the colony as indentured servants, Charles Gordon wrote to his cousin back home, *"If Servants knew what a Countrey this is for them, and that they may live like little [lords] here, I think they would not be so [shy] as they are to come."*

The quality of a servant's life in New Jersey, as elsewhere, depended upon the kindness of his or her master. Masters had the right to beat their servants. They could also sell their servants to another master at will. White servants, however, could one day look forward to being free. In New Jersey, the proprietors gave indentured servants 75 acres (30 ha) when they finished their service. Former servants also received corn, clothing, two hoes, and an ax.

SLAVERY IN NEW JERSEY

Slavery in colonial New Jersey dated back to the earliest Dutch settlers. The Dutch captured slaves from the ships of their enemies, the Spanish, and also brought them from Africa to help build New Netherland. The Dutch used Native American slaves as well, as did later groups of settlers.

When the English took control of New Jersey in 1664, slavery continued. Hundreds of slaves from Africa and the Caribbean passed through Perth Amboy on their way to slave markets in New York and Pennsylvania.

In the 1700s, the number of slaves in New Jersey grew quickly as the need for laborers in the colony increased. By the 1730s, one out of every ten people in East New Jersey was a slave.

There were fewer slaves in West New Jersey, where the farms were smaller and the settlers were generally poorer. The west was also home to many Quakers. As time went on, the Quakers became quite outspoken in their distaste for slavery. At their annual meeting in 1776, the Quakers decided that they would no longer own slaves.

This bill of sale for a slave named Harry documents just one of the many slave purchases in New Jersey during colonial times.

LIVES OF SLAVES

Like servants, slaves performed all types of jobs in New Jersey. In sparsely settled areas, they cleared trees from land, built small farm villages, and worked as domestic servants. In large towns, slaves worked as chimney sweeps, blacksmiths, bakers, coopers, and carpenters.

cooper—a person who makes barrels

John Woolman

Born in New Jersey in 1720, Quaker minister John Woolman grew to detest slavery. As a part-time writer of wills, Woolman refused to sign any documents that included the sale or transfer of slaves. From 1746 until his death in 1772, the Quaker minister traveled throughout the Colonies, preaching against slavery and the mistreatment of Native Americans. Woolman was known as "the Quaker saint." In his journal, he wrote about an encounter with a sick friend:

A neighbor received a bad bruise in his body, and sent for me . . . he desired me to write his will. I took notes, and amongst other things he told me to which of his children he gave his young negro. . . . I wrote his will, save only that part concerning his slave, and carrying it to his bedside read it to him. I then told him in a friendly way that I could not write any instruments by which my fellow-creatures were made slaves, without bringing trouble on my own mind. . . . We then had a serious conference on the subject; at length, he agreeing to set her free, I finished his will.

Most slaves performed farming tasks. In East New Jersey, many worked on big farms in the country, called manors. The slaves were the backbone of these farms. They planted, tended, and picked the crops.

Every part of a slave's life was controlled by the master. Slaves couldn't marry without their master's permission, for example. Slaves could be sold away from their friends and family. Most slaves had very little hope of ever being freed.

Some slaves found ways to protest their condition. They worked slowly, destroyed equipment and crops, or stole animals. Running away was another common way of rebelling. The runaways changed their names, tried to pass as freed slaves, and even faked their own deaths. In the 1700s, newspaper advertisements for escaped slaves, such as this one from the *Pennsylvania Journal* of August 1761, appeared frequently in New York, Pennsylvania, and New Jersey:

> *Run-away from the Subscriber a Negro Man named Quaco about five feet eight inches high. . . . Had on . . . an old Light coloured Coat, old torn shirt, a white Pair of Trowsers . . . and a Pair of light coloured yarn Stockings: The said Negro had an iron Collar with two Hooks to it, round his neck, a pair of Hand-cuffs with a chain to them, six Feet [1.8m] long.*

Slaves who rebelled against their masters or ran away risked grave punishments. They could be branded, whipped, or beaten. Penalties for those helping runaway slaves included stiff fines.

NEW YORK

BORDER AGREED UPON IN 1769

Delaware River

Wallkill River

Hudson River

Paterson

Rockaway

Englewood

Hackensack

Morristown

Hanover

Bergen
(Jersey City)

Lehigh River

Easton

Chatham

Orange

Newark

Turky
(New Providence)

New York

Long Island

Lebanon

Elizabethtown
(Elizabeth)

Whitehouse

Raritan River

Woodbridge

Perth Amboy

PENNSYLVANIA

Somerset

Raritan Bay

New Brunswick

Princeton

Middletown

Shrewsbury

South River

✕
Monmouth

Schuylkill River

Trenton

Bordentown

NEW
JERSEY

Bristol

★ Burlington

River

Philadelphia

Delaware

Woodbury

ATLANTIC OCEAN

Wilmington

Mullicus

Wadling River

New Castle

River

Salem

Maurice River

Great Egg Harbor River

*Little
Egg Harbor*

DELAWARE

Greenwich

Fairfield
(Fairton)

*Delaware
Bay*

Cape May

- - - Present-day state boundary
—— Road
★ Colonial capital
● City
✕ Battle site

miles

0   5   10   20

Roads based on "The State of New
Jersey," Samuel Lewis - 1795

Colony at a Crossroads

NEW JERSEY'S LOCATION *between two key colonial capitals makes it an important crossroads during the 1700s.*

ecause it lay between two of colonial America's major cities, New Jersey became an important crossroads for travelers. People hurrying between New York City and Philadelphia traveled through New Jersey. They used a central corridor that stretched from Perth Amboy to Trenton, a town in western New Jersey located on the Delaware River. Along the way, travelers made use of New Jersey roads, ferries, and bridges. The colony's role as a passage between Philadelphia and New York City created a rise in roadside taverns and inns and led to the improvement of New Jersey roadways.

OPPOSITE: This map shows New Jersey's roads, cities, and towns just before the American Revolution.

GETTING AROUND

The first settlers to arrive in the colony used the pathways blazed by the Lenape people for hunting and trade. These and other early roads were just wide enough to handle travelers on foot or on horseback.

Beginning in the early 1700s, laws were passed to create "common highways" between settlements. The colonial assembly decreed that two men in each town should lay out the roads. The town that got the most benefit from the road was charged with making sure it remained in good condition. Because of the road repair law, New Jersey's roads were in better shape than those in other colonies.

In 1732, New Jersey pioneered the public stagecoach. At first, traveling by stagecoach was uncomfortable. Early stagecoaches had no springs, and travelers were sometimes knocked unconscious during bumpy rides.

As roads improved, stagecoach travel boomed. By 1768, coaches left daily to run between New York and Philadelphia, making stops in New Jersey. At the same time, a stagecoach line between Newark and New York ran four times a week.

Improved roads also meant better mail delivery. In New Jersey's earliest days, mail was usually carried by messengers on horseback. The messengers created their own routes or followed arrows carved in trees by previous mail carriers. Most mail was left at taverns or inns for pickup.

Self-employed mail carriers remained important until after the American Revolution. Toward the end of 1768, for example, Joseph Burwell announced that he would be starting a postal run between Union, New Jersey, and Philadelphia, for one year. Burwell promised to handle his business *"with the greatest Care and Fidelity . . . to those, who are pleased to employ him."*

New Jersey was separated from New York by the Hudson River and from Philadelphia by the Delaware River. Most 18th-century travelers crossed these two major waterways by ferry. The first ferry, which began operating in 1661, connected Bergen to Manhattan Island. At Bergen, the ferry operator was required to keep the boat ready at all times. The price of a routine trip across the Hudson was regulated. At night or in bad weather, however, the ferry operator could charge more. The first ferries, operated by Dutch settlers, were little more than rowboats and flat-bottomed rafts. Later, ferryboats were large enough to carry passengers, cargo, and livestock.

Public stagecoaches began operating in New Jersey in 1732.

TAVERNS

Tavern keepers in the Colonies sometimes hung signs from roadside trees that pointed the way to their establishments in town, as shown in this 1794 painting of Woodbridge, New Jersey.

In 1668, New Jersey passed a law requiring every town to build a tavern to serve travelers. From the colony's earliest days, taverns served an important purpose. They offered weary travelers a place to rest, have some food and drink, and spend the night. The earliest taverns, however, were often unpleasant and uncomfortable. Visitors slept on floors covered with hay. There was often little or no food to be had. As stagecoach lines grew and prospered, the number of taverns also grew, and the quality of the taverns improved.

In the mid-1700s, taverns served as important meeting places where colonists could gather to talk about happenings in the world around them. Here, they could discuss the

Tankard of ale

issues of the day and air their opinions. The tavern was the perfect place to plot riot and rebellion, too.

THE FIGHT FOR LAND

In 1738, Lewis Morris was appointed by the British king to serve as New Jersey's first sole royal governor. Until this time, the colony had shared a governor with New York. Morris, of Monmouth County, was a wealthy landowner. He favored the rights of landowners to collect rent from squatters, people who settled on their land without permission.

Most of the landowners had been given their land by the original proprietors. Many of the squatters, however, viewed themselves as the legal owners of the land they lived on. Although there was an official office in Perth Amboy for the recording of land deeds and claims, it was plagued by so many problems that many people rejected these deeds. County offices experienced the same problems.

Soon after Morris became New Jersey's governor, the wealthy landowners became bolder. Knowing they had the governor's support, they began evicting squatters who refused to pay rent. Some landowners also asked sheriffs to arrest colonists who used the owners' lands without permission.

evict—to remove a tenant by use of a legal procedure

In 1745, Nehemiah Baldwin of Newark was arrested and went to jail for cutting wood on land that a wealthy landowner claimed as his own. Baldwin said that he had purchased the land from the Lenape, but only deeds that had been granted by the proprietors were recognized as valid by New Jersey's colonial government.

Baldwin's arrest sparked a local uprising. His friends attacked the Newark jail and freed him. Several of Baldwin's rescuers were caught and jailed. A mob of armed men rescued the prisoners, then marched through the streets of Newark, attacking the town's militia.

In 1746, evicted squatters armed with clubs and axes banded together. They

militia—a group of citizen-soldiers

ruined crops that they had planted in order to keep the landowners who had evicted them from eating their food. By 1749, about one-third of Essex County was involved in the rioting.

Rich landowners were driven from their land. Officials who were either sympathetic to the rioters or afraid of them refused to bring most of them to trial. Those who were brought to trial were rarely convicted.

Colonists sympathetic or loyal to the landowners were threatened. In 1749, farmer Abraham Phillips was harassed by a group of rioters.

> In the Night 8 or 10 of the Rioters Came to the house of one Abraham Phillips[.] Some broke open his door and Entred his house [and] others pulled of the Roof from his house, they then turned Phillips out of his house threatening him with death.

At the start of the French and Indian War
(1754–1763), these disputes quieted down. The French
and Indian War was the last in a series of conflicts that
were fought between the French and British (and the
Native American allies of each) for control of fur-rich lands
in Ohio and Pennsylvania. At the end of the war, Great
Britain took control of most of Canada and all French
territory east of the Mississippi, except New Orleans.

This woodcut shows Native Americans attacking a log cabin
by night. Such attacks occurred throughout the Colonies during
the French and Indian War.

Amos Roberts

In the early 1740s, Amos Roberts hardly seemed like someone who would lead rioters in a revolt against New Jersey's wealthy landowners. A landowner himself, Roberts and his family lived a comfortable life in Newark. Roberts grew enraged, however, as he watched friends and relatives being ejected from land they had worked and improved. In time, he took on the role of spokesman and leader for discontented colonists.

After leading a 1746 riot in Newark, Roberts traveled throughout northern New Jersey encouraging others to join the cause. In 1748, Governor Jonathan Belcher ordered the rioters' "Chief Captain" to be jailed for high treason—the crime of betraying one's country.

Roberts didn't wait long for rescue. The same day he was locked up, 30 supporters showed up at the Newark jail. They attacked the sheriff, locked his wife in her kitchen, and freed their leader.

As time went on, the number of colonists following Roberts declined. Many felt that he was becoming too powerful. After Roberts's final arrest in 1752, only ten men showed up—days later—to rescue him. He never took part in another riot.

RELATIONS WITH OTHER COLONIES

New Jersey had a history of prickly relations with New York. For many years, both colonies claimed control of territory north of a line that ran from a point on the Delaware River, to a set point on the Hudson River.

The boundary issue was finally settled in New Jersey's favor in 1769. A royal commission decreed that the boundary between the two colonies would be a straight line running from the junction of the Delaware and Neversink Rivers in the northwest to a set point on the Hudson River. Even so, disputes over land ownership along the Hudson continued.

In 1697, New York's royal governor, Richard Coote, Earl of Bellomont, banned the creation of new ports in New Jersey. Any ship that pulled into Perth Amboy before stopping first in New York was to be seized. In July 1698, New York's tax collector tried to seize a ship that docked first at Perth Amboy. He and his helpers were attacked by a mob of club-wielding colonists and then thrown into jail.

Despite these problems, New Jersey carried on a thriving trade with other colonies. By the mid-1700s, the port issues with New York had been resolved. In the 1750s, many goods were shipped out of Cape May, as well as Perth Amboy. These goods included cattle, pork products, animal hides and tallow (fat), cedar, tar, and oysters.

CHAPTER SEVEN

Life in a Prospering Colony

The MID-1700S *prove to be a time of growth and prosperity for New Jersey, as the colony's population booms.*

By the middle of the 18th century, New Jersey was a growing colony. Commerce and industry there were thriving. In 1750, the colony's population was approximately 60,000, lagging behind New York by only about 13,000 colonists.

As New Jersey society became more urban, the clothing worn by both men and women in the colony became more sophisticated. New Jersey women often copied the fashions

OPPOSITE: This woodcut of people in a ballroom in 1700 demonstrates some of the fashions worn by the upper class at that time.

worn by women in Great Britain. In fact, wealthy colonial women imported their clothes straight from Europe.

Wealthy colonists often sat for portraits wearing their finest attire.

For formal occasions, women wore ankle-length gowns made from cotton, silk, and lace. The gown was made up of a skirt and a bodice. A white petticoat, worn beneath the gown, showed through the skirt's open front.

Clothes for everyday use and for working were much simpler. A woman's wardrobe for work might include a plain, ankle-length skirt and bodice. An apron might be worn over the skirt and bodice to protect them from stains.

Colonial undergarments could be painful and bulky. One good example is a set of stays, which were worn by all colonial women. Stays were close-fitting pieces of underwear that could be tightened with laces. They had strips of whalebone or wood sewn into them to make children—even boys—stand up straight and to give grown women a trim, desirable shape. Working women's stays were less stiff than wealthy women's, allowing them greater ease and flexibility. Boots or shoes, gloves, hats, and cloaks completed the colonial costume.

Men wore white linen shirts tucked into short pants called breeches. The calves of the legs were covered by white stockings. Over their shirts, New Jersey men might don long, fitted vests called waistcoats. The waistcoat was an important part of colonial fashion. Upper-class men would never be seen in public without a waistcoat. Working-class men might wear leather vests, aprons, or smocks instead of waistcoats to protect their clothing.

Children dressed like small adults. Girls wore ankle-length gowns and petticoats. Boys wore breeches and shirts.

FUN IN THE COLONY

New Jersey colonists worked hard, but they also enjoyed having fun when the workday was over. One popular pastime was gambling. Colonists held lotteries to raffle off goods, land, and buildings. Although banned in nearby colonies in the 1730s, lotteries remained legal in New Jersey until 1748. As a result, people from other colonies traveled to New Jersey to buy lottery tickets.

Horse racing was another popular form of recreation. One of the earliest racetracks in New Jersey was built at Paulus Hook by Cornelius Van Horst. Other races were held at Perth Amboy and Trenton. People came from miles around to watch the horses and riders compete, and gambling on favorite animals was common.

Horse races could be dangerous. On October 9, 1769, a race at Paulus Hook resulted in an accident, as recorded in an "extraordinary supplement" to the *New York Journal, or, the General Advertiser*: "Mr. Morris Hazard's Horse *Partner*, had the Misfortune in the last Heat to run over a Dog, which occasioned him to fall and throw his Rider, (who was much hurt)."

Another New Jersey pastime was the frolic. Colonists invited their friends and neighbors to help them with spinning, sewing, plowing, chopping wood, or building a new house or barn. Food and drinks were supplied. The frolic lasted until the task was completed.

frolic—a colonial party that combined working and fun

Although colonial children were kept busy with chores and schooling, they also found time for fun and games. In New Jersey and other colonies, toys were handmade. Girls had dolls made out of rags or cornhusks. Boys played with tops carved from pieces of wood or toy houses made out of corncobs. Some colonial games survive to this day, including scotch hoppers (hopscotch), cratch cradle (cat's cradle), and jack straws (pickup sticks).

Patience Lovell Wright

Patience Lovell Wright was born in Bordentown, New Jersey, in 1725 to a Quaker farming family. When she was 44, her husband died, leaving her with five children to support.

Wright turned to sculpting wax figures to earn money. She put together a traveling museum filled with her waxworks and toured throughout the Colonies. In 1772, after the traveling museum was destroyed by fire in New York, Wright moved to England, where she could make more money for her wax sculptures. There, she created life-size figures and busts of politicians, actors, and royalty. Wright's statue of British politician William Pitt still sits in Great Britain's Westminster Abbey.

During the American Revolution, some say that she passed British military secrets to Patriot leaders, hiding the messages in wax figures that she sent to her sister in Philadelphia. Wright died in England in 1786.

EDUCATION

In the mid-1700s, New Jersey had two colleges, a claim that no other colony could make at the time. In 1746, the College of New Jersey, the colony's first university, was founded in Elizabethtown. The college, which admitted only young men, would later move to Newark and then to Princeton. In 1896, the college was renamed Princeton University.

Princeton's GRAMMAR SCHOOL

IN COLONIAL TIMES, A GRAMMAR SCHOOL WAS A PLACE where children went after primary school to learn Latin and other traditional subjects. For this reason, grammar schools were sometimes known as Latin schools. In 1768, a grammar school was opened by the College of New Jersey. An advertisement for new students for the coming school year was sent out at the end of August:

There is a Terrestrial Globe provided for the School, that they may be taught Geography at some Hours of Leisure; they will also have an Hour each Day appropriated to Writing and Arithmetick without any additional Expence, which it is of Importance that they learn early....

In 1752, John Frelinghuysen started a school for ministers in New Brunswick. In 1766, it was renamed Queen's College. Queen's College, like Princeton, was not open to women. In 1825, the college was renamed Rutgers University. Both schools exist today, and both now accept women.

Schooling began at home. Young children were taught the basics of reading and writing by family members. Other lessons might include basic addition and subtraction, as well as learning right from wrong and the skills needed for later in life, such as cooking or sewing for girls and farming for boys.

Around the age of five, some colonial children were sent to dame, or petty, schools. These informal academies were run by neighboring women in their kitchens. In some communities, ministers earned extra money by teaching local children.

Certain groups of settlers did try to provide a more formal education for their children. Puritans in East New Jersey, for example, set aside nontaxable land for schools. Several Dutch and Quaker communities also established schools for their children. Bergen, for example, built a community school as early as 1662. Larger towns were more likely to have such community schools than were rural areas.

A number of New Jersey families, especially those with money, sent their children to be taught at private schools. Philadelphia was known to have many good schools for both boys and girls. Here, students learned reading, writing, grammar, math, Latin, and Greek. Some schools also taught professional skills, such as surveying and bookkeeping, that might allow male students to make a living in the future. This so-called new education was quite a radical idea at the time.

RELIGION IN NEW JERSEY

New Jersey was very tolerant of different Christian religions. As early as 1684, proprietor Gawen Lawrie wrote, *"There be People of several sorts of Religion, but few very Zealous."* Major religious groups included Anglicans, Quakers, Presbyterians, Dutch Reformed, Congregationalists, and Baptists. Most of the residents of East New Jersey were Puritans. They brought their strict rules and beliefs with them to New Jersey.

Elizabethtown's first church, or meetinghouse, was the heart of the community. Announcements of sales, meetings, and other events were posted on the meetinghouse doors. The meetinghouse also served as the town's fort. The cupola was a lookout post. Windows were small and high off the ground.

cupola—a small tower set on top of a roof

Puritan meetinghouses could be uncomfortably cold in winter. Churchgoers brought foot warmers to try to stay warm. A foot warmer was a small device made of stone or iron that could be heated in a fire or have hot coals placed inside. The device was then wrapped in a blanket and carried to church, bed, or anyplace that was cold.

This drawing from around 1740 shows a singing procession of churchgoers.

The minister's sermons could last for several hours. To keep children quiet and adults awake, ushers with long poles roamed the church. Dozing men and children were conked on the head with the knobbed end of the pole; sleepy women were tickled with the squirrel tail that hung from the other end.

The variety of religions in New Jersey reflected the diversity of its people. Despite their different backgrounds and religions, all Jersey colonists worked hard to help the colony grow. Soon, their colonial bonds would be tested by turmoil and violence. 🏵

CHAPTER EIGHT

The Desire for Independence

THE RIFT BETWEEN *England and the Colonies is evident in New Jersey, as Patriot groups form to support rebellion and independence.*

O n the eve of the American Revolution, New Jersey still had one of the smallest populations of any of the British Colonies. Yet the number of colonists had more than doubled since 1750, growing from about 60,000 to nearly 130,000. Most people lived on farms. New Jersey's two capitals of Perth Amboy and Burlington had only about 500 residents each.

In the early 1770s, New Jersey's economy was suffering. New York and Philadelphia still dominated the region's

OPPOSITE: On January 2, 1777, General George Washington led colonial forces, including troops from New Jersey, to victory at the Battle of Princeton. Victories at Princeton and Trenton boosted the morale of Patriots throughout the 13 Colonies.

trade. Land ownership and taxation disputes continued to plague the colony. At a time when New Jersey colonists were looking for someone to blame, increasing problems with Great Britain gave them a target.

Taxation and Trouble

The troubles between England and the Colonies that would eventually lead to the American Revolution began in the 1760s. At that time, Great Britain began to search for ways to recover the money it had spent fighting the French and Indian War. Because the French and Indian War had been fought in America, the British turned to the Colonies to raise money. Parliament (Britain's lawmaking body) began taxing the Colonies.

In 1764, Parliament passed the Sugar Act. The new law placed taxes on sugar, molasses, and other goods brought into the Colonies. A year later, Parliament passed the Stamp Act, which placed a tax on newspapers, legal documents, pamphlets, bills of sale, and even playing cards. It was the first tax that was placed directly on goods produced by the colonists themselves rather than on foreign goods.

People throughout the 13 Colonies gathered in public to protest the act. New Jersey lawmakers sent three representatives to the Stamp Act Congress in New York. Two of these representatives signed a petition asking King George III of England to repeal the Stamp Act. When

Parliament finally put an end to the act in February 1766, people across the Colonies celebrated.

SUPPORTING THE PATRIOTS

British lawmakers soon placed heavy new taxes on certain goods brought into the Colonies, including glass, tea, paper, and lead. The taxes resulted in bad feelings that erupted into violence in early 1770. On March 5, in Boston, Massachusetts, Patriot leaders were whipping up a crowd's emotions against the British. The mob began throwing ice, stones, and other items at British troops. The soldiers shot and killed five of the Patriot rioters. The Patriots dubbed the event "the Boston Massacre."

Patriot—a colonist who favored independence from England

After the killings in Boston, committees of correspondence began to form in Massachusetts. They soon spread to New Jersey and other colonies. These committees were groups of Patriots in charge of sharing information with other colonies. Encouraged by the committees of correspondence, many New Jersey colonists organized a boycott of British goods, including tea.

boycott—an agreement made by a group of people to refuse to purchase goods from a nation or company

New Jersey's first open act of rebellion against Great Britain occurred in November 1774. At the Greenwich Tea Party, 40 men disguised themselves as Native Americans and stole crates of British tea out of a cellar where it was being stored. (Less than a year earlier, Patriots in Boston had held their own tea party.) In Greenwich, the men burned the tea in the streets. Although the owners of the tea wanted the "natives" punished, the tea burners had strong community support. Seven were brought to trial but found not guilty of the charges.

Although New Jersey Patriots joined with those in the other colonies in agitating against British taxes, many acknowledged that their colony was less harmed by the taxes than were some other colonies. In 1764, for example, the New Jersey Committee of Correspondence sent a letter that stated, *"The more Active and Expensive part of the Opposition we expect will be upon the other Colonies who are abundantly more Concerned in Trade, yet it is Necessary so far to Cooperate with them as to Show the Colonies are unanimously of One Mind."*

According to legend, Mary Hays earned the nickname "Molly Pitcher" by carrying water to thirsty soldiers during the Battle of Monmouth in New Jersey in 1776.

On July 4, 1776, five newly appointed representatives from New Jersey were present when the Declaration of Independence was read to the Continental Congress in Philadelphia. This document proclaimed the freedom of the Colonies from England. The following month, all five New Jersey men signed the declaration on behalf of colonists at home.

✠✠✠✠✠✠✠✠ P R O F I L E ✠✠✠✠✠✠✠✠

Jemima Condict

Born in 1754, Jemima Condict spent most of her life on her father's farm near Newark. As a teenager, she began keeping a journal. In 1779, Condict married her cousin, a private in New Jersey's militia.

Condict's journal gives readers a glimpse of life in New Jersey during the Revolutionary War. *"It seems we have troublesome times a coming, for there is a great disturbance abroad in the earth and they say it is tea that caused it,"* she wrote in one entry. *"So then if they will quarrel about such a trifling thing as that, what must we expect but war."* Condict described watching men train for battle, and she mentioned the Boston Massacre. During the war, she wrote about British raids in New Jersey, battles in the region, and the deaths of friends and neighbors.

Condict did not live to enjoy the new liberties that her friends and family members fought so hard to win. In November 1779, she died shortly after giving birth to her first child.

RIGHT: This photograph shows an entry in the journal of Jemima Condict.

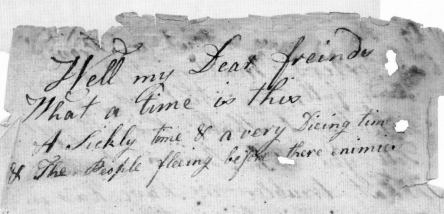

TORIES IN NEW JERSEY

As opposition to England grew throughout the 13 Colonies, New Jersey remained divided. About one-third of the colonists supported the Patriot movement; another third were Tories. The remaining colonists could not decide which side to support.

Tory—a colonist who remained loyal to England; also known as a Loyalist

New Jersey's royal governor, William Franklin, was the son of Patriot leader Benjamin Franklin, whose home was in Philadelphia. In January 1775, William warned New Jersey's assembly that the colony was heading down a road leading to *"Anarchy, Misery, and all the Horrors of a Civil War."* In 1775, after New Jersey received news of the first two battles of the war, at Lexington and Concord in Massachusetts, William Franklin reported to the Earl of Dartmouth that New Jersey colonists were *"arming themselves, forming into Companies, and taking uncommon pains to perfect themselves in Military Discipline."*

During the American Revolution, colonists who stayed loyal to England were often persecuted by others.

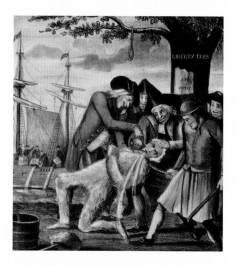

John Malcom, an unpopular commissioner of customs in Boston, is shown being tarred and feathered in 1774.

Some Tories even faced physical assaults. One of the worst types was tarring and feathering. Hot tar was poured over the victim's body, which was then covered with feathers. The hot tar caused painful blisters and was difficult to remove without peeling off layers of skin along with it. Some people nearly died after being subjected to this punishment. A colonial newspaper recounted the fate of one New Jersey Tory:

> Thomas Randolph, cooper, who had publickly proved himself an enemy to his country . . . was ordered to be stripped naked, well coated with tar and feathers and carried in a waggon publickly round the town . . . and as he soon became duly sensible of his offence, for which he earnestly begged pardon, and promised to atone, so far as he was able, by a contrary behaviour for the future, he was released. . . .

THE PRICE OF LIBERTY

Before the American Revolution, New Jersey had been suffering economically. During the war, things got even worse. New Jersey, like other colonies, helped arm and feed the Continental Army. The colony sent iron goods, salt, cloth, and other supplies to the troops. In many cases, the colonists were not paid because the Continental Congress had no cash. British troops from New York caused more problems by raiding New Jersey settlements for food and supplies.

During the war, Perth Amboy was occupied at different times by either British or American troops. Buildings were ruined, citizens were forced from their homes, and the town's economy was devastated.

✳✳✳✳✳✳✳✳✳ P R O F I L E ✳✳✳✳✳✳✳✳✳

William Franklin

Before the American Revolution, William Franklin and his father, Benjamin Franklin, had a close relationship. The relationship between father and son soured in the early 1770s. As royal governor of New Jersey, William remained loyal to the British. In 1775, Benjamin wrote to his son, *"You who are a thorough Courtier see everything with Government Eyes."* William also suffered when his own son sided with his grandfather.

After the war ended, William fled to Britain. From there, he hoped to *"revive that affectionate Intercourse and Connexion which . . . had been the Pride and Happiness of My Life."* Benjamin, however, was unwilling to forgive his son. *"Nothing has ever hurt me so much and affected me with such keen Sensations, as to find myself deserted in my old age by my only son. . . ."* Benjamin Franklin's bitterness toward his son continued until his death in 1790.

New Jersey's location between the British troops occu-
pying New York and those in Philadelphia made the colony
a battleground throughout the war. In the winter of 1776,
writer Thomas Paine described these difficult days for the
Continental Army in New Jersey: *"These are the times that try
men's souls. The summer soldier and the sunshine patriot will, in this
crisis, shrink from the service of their country; but he that stands it now,
deserves the love and thanks of man and woman."* Paine's words
inspired Patriots throughout the Colonies to keep fighting.

In 1781, British forces under General Charles
Cornwallis surrendered to General George Washington
and the Continental Army at Yorktown, Virginia. Two
years later, after a peace treaty had been negotiated, New
Jersey's governor announced that the war was officially
over. On December 18, 1787, New Jersey officials ratified,
or approved, the U.S. Constitution, which laid out the
rules for the new U.S. government.

constitution—the
written set of guiding
laws and principles for a
government, state, or
society

By signing the Constitution, New
Jersey had taken the final step in trans-
forming from a British colony to the third
U.S. state. In the coming decades, as in the
past, New Jersey would continue its
struggle to define itself, finally stepping out of the shadow
of New York and Pennsylvania. As New Jersey continues to
grow and change, it can look back with pride at its history of
rebellion and determination to succeed in the face of all odds,
as well as its colonial roots of tolerance and diversity.

TIME LINE

1524 Sailing for the French, Italian explorer Giovanni da Verrazano explores the New Jersey area.

1609 English explorer Henry Hudson sails along the coast of what is now New Jersey.

1623 Dutch settlers establish Fort Nassau, the first European settlement in New Jersey, at present-day Gloucester City.

1629 The patroon system is established in New Netherland.

1633 The first of several smallpox epidemics kills many Lenni-Lenape.

1643 Settlers from Sweden and Finland establish Fort Elfsborg, near present-day Salem. Nearly all Dutch settlers are driven out of New Jersey by the Lenni-Lenape but return after peace is made.

1655 During the Peach War, Dutch settlers are driven out of New Jersey for the second time by the Lenni-Lenape. The Dutch conquer New Sweden.

1661 The first permanent Dutch settlement is founded at Bergen.

1664 In September, English warships force the Dutch to surrender New Netherland. The English rename parts of the colony New York and New Albania. James, Duke of York, grants an area he names New Jersey to Lord John Berkeley and Sir George Carteret, who become New Jersey's first proprietors.

1668 The General Assembly meets for the first time.

1670 Colonists in eastern New Jersey begin paying a quitrent, or land tax, to the proprietors.

1674 Berkeley sells his interest in New Jersey to two Quakers. Carteret holds the sole interest in the eastern part of the colony.

1676 The colony is split into two colonies, East New Jersey and West New Jersey.

1682 Twenty-four men obtain the rights to East New Jersey, becoming its proprietors.

1700 Riots and violence erupt in East and West New Jersey over land rights and taxes.

1702 Queen Anne of England reunites East and West New Jersey as one royal colony called New Jersey, which shares a governor with New York.

1738 Lewis Morris becomes the first royal governor that New Jersey does not share with New York.

1745 Violence and riots again erupt in response to land ownership disputes in the colony. The unrest continues for nearly a decade.

1746 The College of New Jersey, later renamed Princeton University, is founded.

1754 The French and Indian War begins. It ends nine years later.

1764 Great Britain passes the Sugar Act.

1765 Great Britain passes the Stamp Act.

1766 Queens College receives its charter from the governor. It will later be renamed Rutgers University.

1769 The boundary between New Jersey and New York is officially decided.

1774 New Jersey colonists hold the Greenwich Tea Party to protest English taxes on tea and other goods.

1775 The American Revolution begins in April with the Battles of Lexington and Concord in Massachusetts.

1776 Five representatives from New Jersey to the Continental Congress are among those who sign the Declaration of Independence.

1781 The British surrender to American forces at Yorktown, Virginia.

1783 The American Revolution officially ends with the signing of the Treaty of Paris.

1787 New Jersey is the third state to ratify the U.S. Constitution.

RESOURCES

BOOKS

Hakim, Joy. *A History of US: Making Thirteen Colonies.* New York: Oxford University Press, 2002.

Hodges, Graham Russell, and Alan Edward Brown, eds. *Pretends to Be Free: Runaway Slave Advertisements from Colonial and Revolutionary New York and New Jersey.* New York: Garland Publishing, 1994.

Karlsen, Carol F., and Laurie Krumpacker, eds. *The Journal of Esther Edwards Burr.* New Haven, Conn.: Yale University Press, 1984.

Lukes, Bonnie. *Colonial America.* San Francisco: Lucent Books, 2000.

Myers, Albert Cook. *Narratives of Early Pennsylvania, West New Jersey, and Delaware.* New York: C. Scribner's Sons, 1912.

New Jersey Archives: Extracts from American Newspapers. Trenton, N.J.: John L. Murphy Publishing Company, 1901–1907.

Wood, Peter H. *Strange New Land: Africans in Colonial America.* New York: Oxford University Press, 2003.

WEB SITES

Hangout NJ—Assignment New Jersey—Timeline: http://www.nj.gov/hangout_nj/assignment_timeline.html
The state of New Jersey hosts this special page, with fun facts about the state's history, just for kids.

The Library of Congress Presents America's Story from America's Library: http://www.americaslibrary.gov/cgi-bin/page.cgi
The Library of Congress's Web page for kids contains fascinating information on New Jersey and other American colonies.

New Jersey State Library— New Jersey in the American Revolution, 1763–1783: http://www.njstatelib.org/NJ_Information/Digital_Collections/NJInTheAmerican Revolution1763-1783/index.php
Many primary source documents relating to the American Revolution can be accessed at the state library's Web site.

Rutgers University Cartography— Historical Maps of New Jersey: http://www.mapmaker.rutgers.edu/maps.html
This Web site has an excellent collection of historical maps of New Jersey.

Rutgers University— Women's Project of New Jersey Documents: http://www.scc.rutgers.edu/njwomens history/documents.htm
Excerpts from Jemima Condict's journal and information on women's roles throughout New Jersey's history can be found here.

University of Virginia Library Electronic Text Center— Journal of John Woolman: http://etext.lib.virginia.edu/toc/modeng/public/WooJour.html
This site contains the journal of early Quaker abolitionist John Woolman.

QUOTE SOURCES

CHAPTER ONE

p. 14 "very good land to fall with." http://digilib.nypl.org/dynaweb/hudson/wwm984/@Generic__BookTextView/1947; pt=2039. The New York Public Library Digital Collections. Willis, Nathaniel Parker. *American scenery; or land, lake, and river: illustrations of transatlantic nature*, New York: George Virtue and R. Martin & Company, 1840, p. 130; p. 17 "the grain being dried." Wacker, Peter O. *Land and People: A Cultural Geography of New Jersey*. Trenton, N.J.: New Jersey Historical Commission, 1975, p. 64; p. 18 "the people were about the same." Wacker, p. 72; p. 19 "this day the people of the country." Willis, p. 131; p. 19 "well disposed." Wacker, p. 73; p. 21 "Christians had not only the moral." Wacker, p. 72; p. 22 "Dutch and Sweeds inform us." Wacker, p. 87; p. 24 "they destroy our trade everywhere." Myers, Albert Cook. *Narratives of Early Pennsylvania, West New Jersey, and Delaware*. New York: Charles Scribner's Sons, p. 122; p. 24 "nothing would be better." Wacker, p. 82; p. 26 "poor, sandy, and abominable." Pomfret, John. *Colonial New Jersey: A History*. New York: Charles Scribner's Sons, 1973, p. 21; p. 29 "wretchedly constructed, so close to the fire." Danckaerts, Jasper. *The Journal of Jasper Danckaerts*. New York: Charles Scribner's Sons, 1913.

CHAPTER TWO

pp. 33–34 "shall continue free [citizens]." http://www.cityofjerseycity.org/oldberg/chapter16.shtml. Jersey City History—Old Bergen, Chapter 16; p. 34 "two made coats." *Archives of the State of New Jersey, Volume 1*. Newark: Daily Journal Establishment, 1880, p. 17; p. 35 "the goods to be carried there." http://www.westjerseyhistory.org/books/smith/smithappendix.htm. Smith, Samuel. *The History of Nova Caesaria, or the Colonial History of New Jersey*. Trenton, N.J.: State of New Jersey, 1890; p. 36 "all such as shall settle." *Collections of the New Jersey Historical Society, Volume I*. Newark, N.J.: New Jersey Historical Society, 1875, p. 37; p. 38 "the beastly vice." *The Earliest Printed Laws of New Jersey, 1703–1722*. Wilmington, Del.: Michael Glazier, Inc., 1978; p. 40 "in daytime or at night." Wacker, Peter O. *Land and People: A Cultural Geography of New Jersey*. Trenton, N.J.: New Jersey Historical Commission, 1975, pp. 46–47; p. 41 "the air is very clear, sweet." http://www.swarthmore.edu/SocSci/bdorsey1/41docs/36-tho.html. Thomas, Gabriel. *An Account of West Jersey and Pennsylvania*, 1698; p. 42 "any person or persons." *The Earliest Printed Laws of New Jersey, 1703–1722*, p. 8 and p. 29.

CHAPTER THREE

p. 48 "foundation for after ages." http://www.westjerseyhistory.org/books/smith/smith5.htm. Smith, Samuel. *The History of Nova Caesaria, or the Colonial History of New Jersey*. Trenton, N.J.: State of New Jersey, 1890; p. 51 "not troubled with coughs and head aikes." *Collections of the New Jersey Historical Society, Volume I*. Newark, N.J.: New Jersey Historical Society, 1875, p. 454; p. 51 "the people are generally a sober professing people." http://www.westjersey.history.org/books/smith/smith10.htm. Smith, Samuel. *The History of Nova Caesaria, or the Colonial History of New Jersey*. Trenton, N.J.: State of New Jersey, 1890; p. 52 "one of the best places." *Collections of the New Jersey Historical Society, Volume I*, p. 431; p. 52 "we traveled that day and saw no tame creature." *Collections of the New Jersey Historical Society, Volume I*, p. 125; p. 53 "you cannot come." Wacker, Peter O. *Land and People: A Cultural Geography of New Jersey*. Trenton, N.J.: New Jersey Historical Commission, 1975, p. 39.

CHAPTER FOUR

p. 57 "there are excessive numbers." Wacker, Peter O. *Land and People: A Cultural Geography of New Jersey*. Trenton, N.J.: New Jersey Historical Commission, 1975, p. 45; pp. 59–60 "I know nothing wanting here." *Collections of the New Jersey Historical Society, Volume I*. Newark, N.J.: New Jersey Historical Society, 1875, p. 430–431; p. 60–61 "when I had but one child." Karlsen, Carol, and Laurie Crumpacker. *The Journal of Esther Edwards Burr*. New Haven, Conn.: Yale University Press, 1984, p. 192; p. 62 "the men say that women have no business." Karlsen and Crumpacker; p. 63 "wives are part of the house." Wadsworth, Benjamin. *The well-ordered family: or, Relative duties*. Boston: B. Green, for Nicholas Buttolph, 1712; p. 65 "I watched with Mr. Burr last night." Karlsen and Crumpacker, p. 192; p. 65 "both few and evil." Evans, Elizabeth. *Weathering the Storm*. New York: Charles Scribner's Sons, 1975, p. 45.

CHAPTER FIVE

p. 69 "if servants knew." *Collections of the New Jersey Historical Society, Volume I*. Newark, N.J.: New Jersey Historical Society, 1875, p. 455; p. 72 "a neighbor received a bad bruise." Mott, Amelia Gummere. *The Journal and Essays of John Woolman*. New York: Macmillan, 1922, p. 180; p. 73 "run-away from the subscriber." Hodges, Graham Russell. *"Pretends to Be Free."* New York: Garland Publishing, 1994, p. 89.

CHAPTER SIX

p. 77 "with the greatest care." New Jersey Archives, *Extracts from American Newspapers*, 1768; p. 80 "in the night." Wacker, Peter. *Land and People: A Cultural Geography of New Jersey*, Trenton, N.J.: New Jersey Historical Commission, 1975, p. 351.

CHAPTER SEVEN

p. 88 "Mr. Morris Hazard's horse." New Jersey Archives, *Extracts from American Newspapers*, 1769; p. 90 "there is a terrestrial globe." *Documents Relating to the Colonial History of the State of New Jersey, Volume XXVI*. Paterson, N.J.: The Call Printing and Publishing Company, 1904, p. 269; p. 92 "there be people." http://www.westjerseyhistory.org/books/smith/smith10.htm. Smith, Samuel. *The History of Nova Caesaria, or the Colonial History of New Jersey*. Trenton, N.J.: State of New Jersey, 1890.

CHAPTER EIGHT

p. 98 "the more active and expensive." http://www.njstatelib.org/NJ_Information/Digital_Collections/NJInTheAmericanRevolution1763-1783/1.2.pdf. Gerlach, Larry R., ed. *New Jersey in the American Revolution, 1763–1783: A Documentary History*. New Jersey Historical Commission; p. 99 "it seems we have troublesome times." Evans, Elizabeth. *Weathering the Storm*. New York: Charles Scribner's Sons, 1975, p. 36; p. 100 "anarchy, misery." http://www.njstatelib.org/NJ_Information/Digital_Collections/NJInTheAmericanRevolution1763-1783/4.2.pdf. *Votes and Proceedings, January 11–February 13, 1775 (Burlington, 1775)*, pp. 5–7; p. 100 "arming themselves, forming into companies." Gerlach, Larry R. *Prologue to Independence*. New Brunswick, N.J.: Rutgers University Press, 1976. p. 263; p. 101 "Thomas Randolph, cooper." http://www.njstatelib.org/NJ_Information/Digital_Collections/NJInTheAmericanRevolution1763-1783/5.16.pdf. *Archives of the State of New Jersey*. Newark, N.J.: Daily Advertiser Printing House, 1886, p. 591; p. 102 "you who are." Bruce, William Cabell. *Benjamin Franklin, Self-Revealed: A Biographical and Critical Study Based Mainly on His Own Writings, Volume 1*. New York: Putnam, 1917, p. 40; p. 102 "revive that affectionate intercourse." Herbert, Eugenia W., and Claude-Anne Lopez. *The Private Franklin: The Man and His Family*. New York: Norton, 1975, p. 256. p. 102 "nothing has ever hurt." *The Private Franklin: The Man and His Family*, pp. 257–258. p. 103 "these are the times." http://www.bartleby.com/73/1821.html. Paine, Thomas. "The Crisis," no. 1. Conway, Moncure D., ed. *The Writings of Thomas Paine, Volume 1*, 1894, p. 170.

INDEX

ABOUT THE AUTHOR AND CONSULTANT

ROBIN DOAK is a writer of fiction and nonfiction books for children, ranging from elementary to high school levels. Subjects she has written on include American immigration, the 50 states, American presidents, and U.S. geography. Doak is a former editor of *Weekly Reader* and has also written numerous support guides for educators. She holds a Bachelor of Arts degree in English, with an emphasis on journalism, from the University of Connecticut and lives in Portland, Connecticut.

BRENDAN McCONVILLE is currently a professor in the Department of History at Boston University where he teaches courses on colonial America, the American Revolution, and American Politics. He received his Ph.D. from Brown University. McConville has written numerous books and articles on the early years of the American colonies, including *These Daring Disturbers of the Public Peace: The Struggle for Property and Power in Early New Jersey*. He is also the consultant for *Voices from Colonial America: Massachusetts* and resides in Boston.

ILLUSTRATION CREDITS

Cover, title page, page 17:
Picture Collection, The Branch Libraries, The New York Public Library, Astor, Lenox and Tilden Foundations

Pages 9, 32, 43, 58, 64, 66, 68, 100, 102:
The Granger Collection

Pages 11, 46, 50, 71, 72, 78, 87, 99:
From the Collection of the New Jersey Historical Society

Pages 12, 44, 54, 77, 81, 84:
North Wind Picture Archives

Page 23:
© CORBIS

Pages 26, 30, 56, 94:
Bridgeman Art Library

Pages 48, 49:
© Gianni Dagli Orti/CORBIS

Pages 86, 89:
Art Resource

Page 93:
© Bettmann/CORBIS

Page 98:
Louis S. Glanzman, National Geographic Society

End sheets, 8, 37:
The Library of Congress